The Empath Survival Guide

The Complete Strategies For Highly Sensitive People.

How to Learn to Manage Your Emotions, Overcome Anxiety and Fears, Learn Protection Techniques from Energy Vampires

By Daniel Travis Cooper

Table of Contents

Introduction

Congratulations on purchasing *The Empath Survival Guide: The Complete Strategies for Highly Sensitive People. How to Learn to Manage your Emotions, Overcome Anxiety and Fears, Learn Protection Techniques from Energy Vampires* and thank you for doing so.

The following chapters will discuss what empaths are, what makes them unique, how to manage your emotions, how to overcome those feelings of anxiety, how to manage your abilities as an empath, how to protect yourself from energy drainers, and even parenting tips for children with these abilities!

There are plenty of books on this subject on the market, thanks again for choosing this one! Every effort was made to ensure it is full of as much useful information as possible, please enjoy!

Chapter 1: What is an Empath?

The Definition of Empathy

The basic definition of empathy is the capacity or ability to understand what someone is experiencing and to understand how that affects them emotionally. There are many situations in which this can come into use, and empathy can manifest in a number of different ways. When someone is empathetic, what people generally mean is that the person can put themselves in someone else's shoes, so to speak. This means they can see things as the other person would anticipate the feelings that person would have about the circumstances, and they can know—to some extent—how the person would react to certain situations and stimuli.

Someone who has a decent amount of empathy will often say things like, "this must be hard for you," "I know what you're going through," or "I know how hard this must be," they really do mean it. They understand how hard that emotional impact must be, and they understand what it must feel like to be in your position. An empath will have an even greater understanding of this, as someone who feels empathy for you has theoretically stepped into your position and felt it for themselves. Typically, when someone who has a very high empathetic response senses that someone near them is going through something difficult, it can be very difficult for them not to say anything to the person who is suffering.

In short, they see that pain and they feel compelled to do something to address, fix, or alleviate it in some way. In some cases, this can be overstepping bounds, or it might not be received well by the person who is suffering. It's important to maintain boundaries with the people around you, in spite of how strongly you might feel about what they're dealing with.

While these aspects of empathy are typically discussed or understood, there are some aspects that may be less commonly understood. There are three subcategories of empathy that can lead to different results and which are triggered differently. It's possible for one empath or empathetic person to exhibit all three types, as they're not mutually exclusive.

While empathy is something that occurs naturally in some measure to most people, it and its components can be strengthened or honed. As emotional intelligence increases and as you increase your understanding of the mechanics of empathy, you will be able to make them work for you with greater frequency and success.

Cognitive

Cognitive empathy gives you an insight into the thoughts and feelings of others that can sometimes seem like mind reading. As it happens, this ability is less like mind reading and more like anticipation through emotional understanding. Most people understand that behind every emotion, there is a logical conclusion that triggers it and a logical conclusion that is formed because of it. This type of empathy gives you a clear enough insight into what another person is feeling, that you can put yourself in their shoes and more or less see what they're going to do next.

At first, when one thinks about this mechanism, it can seem somewhat like something out of a detective novel or a mystery drama. However, it really does come down to knowing what that person is feeling and how, if it were you, it would lead you to feel. People also often have behavior patterns that are harder for them to see, as they're too close to them. Someone experiencing cognitive empathy can often plot the mental course someone will take and see what the next steps will be.

This will be more common between people who know one another, as more time with the person will lead to a better basis for predicting future behaviors.

You won't typically have situations that are as miraculous as those in your average mystery novel centered around a genius detective.

One of the many benefits of this particular type of empathy is being aware of what someone will be able to handle or deal with. This is a particularly useful trait in someone who is leading others or who is working in a position of authority. If you are aware of someone's emotional capacity to handle certain things, you can more appropriately assign a workload that won't overwhelm or underwhelm them.

There are many situations in which this type of empathy can be quite beneficial. Try to think up some of them and how you could use this ability in your life.

Emotional

The most common thing associated with empathy is emotions. This is because emotional empathy is an emotion of its own. This type of empathy is also known as *affective empathy* or *automatic empathy*. This is because the response of tuning into the emotions of others and the capacity to develop sympathy or compassion based on that is a natural urge that many people feel. It's sort of the emotional basis for those two more complex actions.

Let's define compassion and sympathy in order to make a distinction between empathy, sympathy, and compassion.

Empathy – The ability to understand and share the sentiments or feelings of another.

Sympathy – Feelings of pity or sorrow at the misfortunes of another.

Compassion – Leniency, and concern for the sufferings of others.

You can see, by these definitions, how these things are interconnected. You can also see, based on the definitions listed above, that these three things are distinctly different from one another. Seeing the connection between these whiles being able to differentiate between them is important to being able to master them and use them to your advantage.

In addition to the above, there are three parts to the emotional empathy response that you may recognize:

1. Having an emotional response with yourself that fits what someone else is going through.
2. Feeling distressed as a response to the difficulties being experienced by someone else.
3. Feeling compassion for the person who is going through something.

One of the things you will notice is the difference between feeling distress as you own emotional response to the situation in front of you and picking up on the emotions of the person you're dealing with or talking to.

Compassionate

While being compassionate can be a response to feeling empathy for someone, *compassionate empathy* is its own subcategory. When one feels the compassionate empathetic response, one is often compelled to do something to help alleviate the pressure, stress, difficulty, or misfortune of another. This can also be seen as the Good Samaritan response, the helpful response, and the volunteer response. It's seen as selfless, altruistic, helpful, kind, and it's held as a virtue among many people in societies around the world.

Empathy is something that can come up in a lot of different situations, and it's one that can vastly improve a good number of them as well. Can you think of a situation in which a little bit of empathy would have made things go more smoothly?

What is an Empath?

To put it in as few words as possible: most people have empathy and a very small percentage of people are empaths.

Being an empath means that you're exceptionally sensitive to the emotions and feelings of the people in your life and in your environment. There are quite a few traits of an empath that are quite specific. For many empaths, you might have had no answer for these traits, habits, or behaviors of yours until you realize that they're part of what makes an empath so special.

Being an empath is something that consumes many—if not all—corners of your life. There are very few habits, interactions, abilities, or traits that aren't affected in some way by one's empathic tendencies. These abilities and characteristics, in large measure, can be improved, strengthened, and honed once one has achieved an understanding of them and once one knows the situations in which they can be quite useful.

It's important to be aware that while empaths have some traits of their own that are there from birth or a very young age, those traits are not *skills*. Those are *talents*; they need to be honed and you need to flex those muscles in order for those talents to turn into skills. The sensitivities that we have are simply that, and they can't be removed. They can, however, be perfected.

An empath will always have a certain sensitivity to the things going on around them, but the things that they do with those sensitivities will determine whether they become annoyances or skills. As you gain practice with the skills to which you're predisposed, using them will require less effort.

The different types of empath could be listed out in their specificity, but a more accurate representation would be a very large, very odd-looking Venn diagram. There are so many different ways in which someone can be in tune with the people around them and there are many people who experience or exhibit the characteristics of several different types of empaths.

This can make it quite difficult for someone to look at a list of the different "types of empath," in the hopes to put a label on the types of abilities they have. The most effective way to understand yourself as an empath is to get the information on what the most common traits of empaths are, see which of those traits you see within yourself, and work on honing the skills while working to diminish the drawbacks that can come with being highly sensitive.

As for the subject of a label, it might be easiest to avoid using one for the time being. If having that distinction is important to you, being able to say that you're an empath or a highly sensitive person with intuitive abilities is an ideal broad-stroke description for it.

I've listed the most commonly shared traits of empaths here so you can take a look and see if these fit you. If you find that you identify with a good number of these, you might be an empath. Don't despair however, if there are some items in this list that just aren't you.

We are all unique people with unique tendencies and abilities. You can be an empath without having all of these traits. If you find that you don't have a lot of these abilities, but you do have some, it can indicate a higher level of empathetic sensitivity that is somewhere between basic empathy and highly sensitive. There is absolutely nothing wrong with either outcome.

1. Strong emotional content on television has a profound impact on you.

   The thing about being in tune with the emotions and suffering of other people is that it isn't limited to the people that you can touch. It's not limited to the people that are right in front of you.

   Thanks to the digital age we currently live in, many of our friends and family are only accessible by a digital means. Because of this, our empathy is forced onto those channels and we learn how to pick up on the things that someone is thinking or feeling through that lens.

   This could be a reason why seeing someone dealing with something on screen, in text, in movies, in pictures, etc., still, affect us in a very real and very monumental way at times.

2. People are always asking you for advice.

   Empaths often conduct them in such a way that signals other people as to our abilities. Thanks to this, people tend to know that they can rely on us to provide sound advice, or at the very least, lend an ear.

   Think of it like having an invisible, yet perceivable beacon over your head that flashes, telling people that you know how to give great advice.

   One of the things about this particular ability that required the practice and honing that I mentioned, is being able to rely on yourself for advice. Many empaths struggle with being able to analyze the problems of others and give sound, usable advice while struggling with their own problems. Perhaps even more frustrating is that many of these problems are usually similar in nature to those that we've solved for others.

   This is where that practice really comes in handy. We'll explore this in the exercises and journal prompts given in this book.

3. Intimate relationships can overtake all of your thinking and the energy you get from them flows throughout your entire life.

I'd like to start by saying that starting and cultivating meaningful personal relationships as an empath is absolutely possible. There are things to consider, to be certain.

For instance, it should be noted that someone who is empathic will often have the need to discuss problems as they occur and resolve them on a fairly immediate basis. Someone who has a "wait and see," method of resolving problems would often cause severe anxiety in this type of person. This is not always the case, but it is quite common.

The emotional energy that an empath picks up from the people around them has a fairly profound effect on them and it can tend to envelop the empath's entire thought process if they are concerned enough with it.
Thanks to this, being closely involved with someone can seem overwhelming or like it's putting so much accessible emotion into their life that it can permeate every aspect of the person's life.

This is what makes boundaries in personal relationships so important. As an empath, you would do well to insist on a physical space where you can be on your own, and where the emotions of others, no matter how connected they are to you, may not enter. Personal boundaries will give you space in your life to get a reprieve and do the things you need to heal, recuperate, grow, and flourish.

4. Your sensitivity could be mislabeled as anxiety or shyness.

People who are very sensitive can get overwhelmed, we can feel like we need to recuse ourselves from the company of others, and we can seem a little bit edgy at times. There are more aspects to this, but it gives you a general idea of how these labels can be put on us, in spite of being quite healthy.

Finding the right fulfillment, boundaries, spaces, and people can work wonders for the emotional, physical, and mental health of an empath.

5. Regardless of introversion or extroversion, you withdraw often.

This doesn't mean you are particularly a wallflower at social gatherings, but it could mean that you find yourself taking a couple of days to stay in rather than going out. It could mean that you take some time to read instead of going to a concert, or that you cancel plans you thought you'd be able to keep.

To take time for yourself is healthy, but one must do so in a measure that doesn't cut one off from the people and the world around one.

6. When thinking of leadership roles, you always assume that means putting the team first.

As an empath, you see the role of leadership as being a role in which you are completely responsible for the well-being and the success of your team. People who are otherwise focused might see leadership as an opportunity to get things from others, or to take credit for the work that is done by their team. Such things would rarely occur to an empath, which often contributes to their being such effective and admirable leaders.

7. The world you've created in your mind is rich and vibrant.

People who are empathic tend to spend a lot of time thinking, daydreaming, hypothesizing, thinking up hypothetical situations, and putting together characters and stories. Thanks to this, we have a very rich and vibrant environment in our minds.

8. Others find your very presence to be calming.

    Thanks to your abilities, you often know what energies to give off in order to make someone feel at ease. This will draw people to you or make it very easy for people to relax around you.

    Sometimes, the best compliment you can be paid is for someone with severe insomnia to say they got their best sleep in days, simply because you stayed the night with them.

9. Hunger very quickly turns into anger, sometimes even before hunger.

    Thanks to your heightened sensitivity to feelings, urges, inclinations, and the things going on in your body, your blood sugar can crash a little more quickly than it can for some of the others around you. If you find yourself getting "hangry," with any sort of frequency, try keeping a granola bar or some other snack in your bag for times when things really start to bear down on you.

    Keeping yourself fed can also help to lessen the effects and frequency of sensory overload.

10. You're highly sensitive to wardrobe malfunctions.

Things like scratchy fabrics, stiff tags, tight underwear, wrinkly socks, and loose waistbands can tend to bother you throughout your entire day. Many people have the ability to simply tune out the annoyance of such things as this, but those who are highly sensitive may have less of an ability to do something like this to get through their day.

A good rule to live by when you're getting dressed is that if it bothers you a little bit while you're getting ready in the morning, it will bother you ten times more once you're in public.

Try to go with clothes that fit well, fabrics that are comfortable and breathable, and socks whose elastic is still working quite well.

11. Criticism is painful beyond reason.

Even if the person who is offering the criticism is going so out of a concern for you and the desire to help you to improve, it can feel like a slap in the face when the answer isn't automatic approval.

12. You feel an overwhelming love for pets, animals, or babies.

    You might find babies, animals, and cute things to be *so* cute that it's overwhelming. You might get so excited when there is a baby or an animal in your presence, that nothing else matters or even registers with you. This is a common trait for an empath to have.

    Since empaths are more receptive to beauty and innocence, babies and animals check both of these boxes and stand out to empaths for these reasons.

13. You're exceedingly perceptive and minor details don't escape you easily.

    Thanks to your sensitivity to certain things and your ability to pick up on the things around you, you could be pretty detail oriented. You could find that this eye for detail is an extreme advantage in the workplace.

14. You're prone to jumping or startling easily.

    There is often a lot going on in the mind of an empath. Due to this, it is easy for a sudden noise or loud jolt to affect you a little bit more than some others might be.

15. Once startled, you may be shaken for a while or experience "aftershocks."

Sometimes, after we get startled, we can notice little shivers or quakes throughout bodies after we've been through a loud startle or scare. This is your body anticipating another scare and letting off energy that it's building up to stave off danger.

Take some time to close your eyes, relax, focus on the immediate environment, and get yourself ready to deal with the things that you're working on. Most startles won't happen again!

16. Stimulants are very effective in short measure.

Caffeine hits fast and it hits hard for some empaths. Coffee can be used sparingly and to a very effective result.

17. Depressants are very effective in short measure.

Things like alcohol hit very quickly and very hard. It's best to use alcohol sparingly, and it's best to drink in moderation.

18. It's easy for you to get a feel for where someone is coming from when telling you something.

For instance, when someone approaches you about a situation, you might immediately get an inkling for what they're about to say about it. It's important to hear people out and let them tell you everything they have to say, even if you think you know what they'll say.

19. You do a lot of introspection and deep thinking.

There is a lot to process when so many emotions and thoughts are passing through your mind over the course of your day. It makes sense that you would need to take time to sift through all of them and process the important parts. Just take care not to do this in the middle of social interactions or meals with others!

20. Pain sets in more easily.

Being highly sensitive dials up the volume on so many things. Unfortunately, this can also affect your threshold for physical pain.

21. You ask the big questions in life and seek a lot of answers about the status quo.

People who have so many thoughts and feelings passing through their minds throughout the day have the capacity and the thirst to know more things about life, each other, and the way things are.

Empaths will often find themselves looking for answers to questions that others might not even think to ask.

22. You find cruelty and violence to be abhorrent.

Empaths are exceedingly receptive to the feelings of others and are very sensitive to seeing things of a violent or harmful nature happening to the people around us. Our empathic abilities tend to make us feel the things that we watch people going through in our environment. It's best to remove yourself from these situations if at all possible.

23. You feel ailments or illnesses as someone you love is going through them.

This trait is one that can be seen as a downside. Because of how sensitive we are to the struggles and emotions of the people around us that we can actually develop an illness or a condition that is being experienced by someone near us.

Compartmentalization is important for this reason and being stronger about what you allow to affect you is a skill that will help with this.

24. Deadlines and time limits leave you feeling shaken or rattled.

Keeping to deadlines and time constraints isn't necessarily difficult for you to do from a work effort standpoint. However, you might find that time limits on things tend to make you feel more harried, pressured, and less effective. It can seem like all the energy you originally had to work on your project is completely occupied by the time limit that's been imposed on you.

Things you should have easily been able to achieve otherwise, seem to be slammed up against that timeline and can only be accomplished with stress, a furrowed brow, and terrible personal care practices.

Don't allow yourself to skip meals to get to those deadlines; you need to eat, sleep, bathe, and breathe. Let yourself do those things.

25. Your greatest efforts are expended on not messing up.

Being so concerned with the task of not messing up is essentially a recipe for how to mess up. Relax, take a deep breath and focus on doing your best. Don't allow this sensitivity to dictate the quality of your work or the richness of your social interactions.

26. Change is jarring or even upsetting.

Due to the empath's sensitivity to the things in their environment and all the small details, large changes or shifts can be jarring or upsetting for an empath. Knowing the changes are coming and having input on what those changes will be, does wonders to help the empath to adjust to changes, or to feel calmer when those changes take effect.

27. You find yourself feeling exhausted after having absorbed and processed the feelings of others.

Feeling your emotions requires a level of energy to be spent throughout each day. Feeling the emotions of several others in your day requires that many more times that amount of energy and it can exhaust you so much more quickly than you may realize.

This is part of what makes it so important to take time for yourself and do the things you know you need to do to recharge your batteries.

28. Sensory overload is much more easily achieved.

Unfortunately, with how sensitive we can be to every detail, every emotion, every bad vibe and more around us, it can be easy for all of it to reach a boiling point. When someone experiences sensory overload, there is a very strong inclination to just shut it all down, put hands over the ears, stop in their tracks, and just wait out the feeling of overwhelm.

This can, like many things, also be experienced in a number of different ways. What's important is that when sensory overload strikes, you come up with an exit strategy. You're able to calm your breathing, focus on one thing, or leave the area until you're able to calm down and resume what you're doing.

Shopping in malls or grocery stores is a pretty commonplace for such a thing to occur, as well as concerts, public transport, or busy restaurants.

29. You are affected by the general atmosphere of a room or "vibe."

"Vibe" may seem like a bit of a vague descriptor for the general feeling in the atmosphere of a place or person. However, what we mean is that certain emotions will leave a residual feeling in the room, and you will find yourself being affected by that from time to time.

For instance, have you ever walked into a room with a couple of people in it and gotten the feeling that someone was very upset or angry? That would be an example of the vibe of a room affecting you.

30. Beauty moves you deeply, sometimes to tears.

Beauty is all around us in the world. One of the benefits of being an empath is that that beauty isn't lost on us. We don't find ourselves missing out on how beautiful the things around us are and we don't let it pass us by.

When we allow ourselves to fully experience the beauty of the things around us, it can be a very moving experience and we can feel a very strong connection to that beauty.

31. You tend to adopt the feelings of others and feel them as though they're your own.

This is one of the more basic traits of an empath. Feeling the emotions and feelings that someone we care about or someone in our immediate vicinity is feeling. This comes along with the compulsion to want to help those people to sort through those feelings and work them out.

This is partially a self-preservation tactic, and partially a tactic that is done out of love for the people around us.

However, you do things, make sure you're taking care of yourself as well.

32. Conflict can make you physically ill.

Knowing that there is unrest in your immediate vicinity or with someone that you care about can give you knots in your stomach, headaches, or even cold symptoms.

This is part of what makes us want to resolve things as soon as they come up. The longer we let them sit, the worse we tend to feel.

Resolving conflicts is one of the sharpest skills an empath can have, and I dare say this is out of self-defense and the need to survive more than anything else. Caring for the people involved in the conflict and wanting to help them feel better is a very close second.

33. You cannot see someone who needs help without desperately wanting to provide it.

Empaths have a very strong reflexive response called *compassionate empathy*. It means that when we see something wrong for someone, we roll up our sleeves, jump in, and take care of it. This is not always the best course of action.

People do need to learn how to solve their own problems in life, and people need to be able to do so without your assistance. You can't resolve the issues of everyone in your life, at every hour of the day.

If you did, when would you sleep? Eat? Work? Have fun? There would be no time left for you or your needs in the day. This is why it's so important to make sure we're spending our time as wisely as possible.

34. Occasionally, you will feel overwhelming emotions that are seemingly "out of nowhere."

This is one of the more basic traits of an empath. Feeling the emotions and feelings that someone we care about or someone in our immediate vicinity is feeling. It is possible for us to be minding our own business at the gym, the mall, on the bus, or at the store when we suddenly get unreasonably angry with no understanding of why.

It can be incredibly disruptive, and it can be exceedingly alarming to the people around us who aren't sure where any of it even came from.

As we hone our skills and we get better a identifying the types of emotions we can pick up on from those around us, it can give us a better sense of control on them and can help us to know which emotions are really our own and which ones we're just borrowing for a moment.

35. It's very hard for people to lie to you.

Lies come with a lot of little details attached to them. From the little twitches that people have that tell you they're being dishonest, to the things that would make the lie make less sense, we are drawn to these little details.

As empaths, being made aware of small details makes it harder to just accept that things could happen to line up in a certain way and that the story went the way it was told, in spite of inconsistencies.

Detecting lies and being an intuitive response that tells you something is wrong, are things that come with being an empath. Listen to those feelings, as they're often correct.

36. You have a "big heart," and will often give too much of yourself.

In general, people with empathic abilities can tend to be kinder and more forgiving than people with a basic level of empathy. As a result of this, we can tend to give more of ourselves to the people around us who need it.

It's possible for someone with heightened sensitivity to lessen their own needs and put the needs of others in front of their own. As a result of this, the empath will find themselves more frequently exhausted, stressed, and even feeling neglected because no one is taking care of them the way they are taking care of others.

It is imperative that the average empath set boundaries for what they can give to others and keep to them. This way, they will be able to ensure they always have enough energy for the things they need, as well as the things they want to do to help other people in their lives.

Give some of yourself, but not all.

37. You seem to be a walking target for "energy vampires."

Energy vampires have a very difficult time creating energy on their own. They have a difficult time generating positivity, staying productive, keeping their energy levels high, and they very rarely (if ever) give others energy.

Because of their dearth of energy, they tend to suck it from the people around others, using it to stay alive, upright, and somewhat happy. Some energy vampires know that they're doing what they're doing. Some are completely oblivious.

Thanks to the energy that you naturally give others, people who are looking for that kind of arrangement will find themselves drawn to you. The energy that you exude and the positivity that you instill in others is something they crave.

It would be prudent for the average empath to avoid this sort of person.

38. You feel that you know, without asking, what is going on around you.

Being able to pick up on the vibe in the room around you or pick up on the emotions and inklings of the people around you gives you a general idea of what is going on before you even ask. You might find that you have the uncanny ability to predict the outcome of the situation in front of you, or what someone is about to tell you as a result of this.

39. You're an effective communicator and listener.

Talking with others and listening to what they have to say is, for some empaths, a joy. Connecting with people, listening to what they have to say, and talking about the things that you both have in common can give the empath a lot of fulfillment and enjoyment.

As such, you tend to listen to what the other person says with a genuine interest and acknowledge the things that they say to you in a way that lets the other person know you're actively listening. This is not as common a trait as it could be and when people find it in others, they tend to really enjoy it.

Not all conversations and conversationalists are the same, and some are more enriching than others!

40. You have mood swings.

Being sensitive to emotion and susceptible to feeling a wide range of them can mean that your mood seems to be all over the place. It's important to take stock of things when your mood changes, ask yourself what caused the change, assess if the emotion is yours and is appropriate and move forward accordingly.

As you gain more practice with this, the process will go more and more smoothly, and you will have an easier and easier time with it.

41. You have a trustworthy magnetism.

Being great at communicating makes people feel more open with you. This is part of seeming more honest and trustworthy. People who clam up or don't talk as much, or who can't keep a conversation going can tend to keep people from feeling comfortable or at ease with them.

You will often find that you're the person that someone asks to keep an eye on their laptop while they go to the bathroom at Starbucks, hold their place in line, or help them with something on the street.

42. You might reach for addictive substances to escape the other traits of an empath.

There is no question that the average empath has a lot of things to bear and that there is a lot of stress that can be involved with that. Unfortunately, with this territory and with the heightened sensitivity about the things going on around you, addictive substances can have more of a draw or more of an appeal.

If you're using such a thing as a crutch or as an escape, it is advised that you seek help to stop or that you find other ways to support you through the tough times that won't do damage after continues use or practice.

43. You're very creative.

The empath's capacity for detail, beauty, original thought, and imagination create a perfect storm for creativity. Many people who feel very deeply or who are perceptive of the feelings of others will turn out to be quite creative with some medium or another.

If you haven't looked into this for yourself, consider looking into some creative means that interest you and see how you like it!

44. Clutter and a crowded space make you uneasy or stressed.

Your mental space has so much going on and going through it with great regularity. Thanks to this, physical clutter around you tends to send your mind into a flurry much more quickly than it might do for others around you. The need for an open, clean, orderly space is justified when so much is going on internally.

How is Having Empathy Different from Being an Empath?

Having empathy is a natural brain response to stimuli in the environment around you. We will cover more about this at the end of this chapter. Empathic abilities, however, are something a little bit stronger. They are characterized by a much stronger response in that same portion of the brain, and by traits that otherwise suggest a very high sensitivity to energies and other sensations around the empath.

Having no empathy, however, is a characteristic of some mental disorders and warrants the consultation with a medical professional. If you find that you have little to no empathy for the people around you, you may want to speak with your doctor about what that could mean for your mental health.

Where Does Empathy Come From?

Empathy is a concept that wasn't really on the radar of mental health professionals until as late as the 1950s. Once it was discovered, however, research was being conducted in large numbers. It was discovered in some of the most recent research and experimentation on the subject, that empathy is formed in the right supramarginal gyrus of the brain. There are other portions of the brain that are active and affected in the process, but the right supramarginal gyrus seems to be the key to the whole puzzle.

Interestingly, it was found that the right supramarginal gyrus doesn't have time to kick in and make us act with empathy in situations that involve quick thinking or snap decisions. That's why our empathetic and considerate responses tend to be dramatically reduced if not completely inhibited in such cases.

The right supramarginal gyrus seems to be the part of the brain that allows us to specifically compare the circumstances and situations someone else is dealing with, to our own. It allows us to simulate the emotional responses that would be appropriate in someone else's situations so that we can feel it for ourselves.

It's when this portion of the brain that is underperforming or performing at very low levels that people seem to be incapable of feeling enough empathy for the people around them. This was found to be true in several studies of people who had been diagnosed with psychopathy, a condition characterized by little to no empathy.

Chapter 2: Understanding Energy

Different Types of Energies

When dealing with the energies that people have, there are three categories that are somewhat broad. You will find that each of these types of energy covers a wide range of things for which the energy can be used, what affects them, how they're generated, and more. Let's take a look at the three categories, what they cover, and how to differentiate between them.

Physical Energy

Physical energy is probably the most commonly thought-of when people talk about having the energy to deal with and to do certain things. Physical energy is a basic energy, as it keeps you moving, gives you the ability to sit upright, to take the stairs instead of the elevator, and everything else that you do physically each day.

There are ways to increase your physical energy, like eating more protein-rich foods, getting sufficient rest each night, taking a walk, exercising to increase your energy over time, and more. I'm sure you've heard of doing these things to help you to get through your day! There are more chemical, short term means like caffeine, which will give you a boost in your physical energy for a short time, but the dependence on this over time will only serve to cut down on your capacity for physical energy and will lessen the ease with which you can create it on your own over prolonged periods of usage.

Emotional Energy

Emotional energy is the stuff that makes it possible for you to deal with the things that go wrong or badly. This energy can be replenished by feeling positive emotions and experiencing things that make you feel positive emotions.

If someone is low on emotional energy, they may be less able to deal with the impact of someone telling them about their day, about the things that have gone wrong, or with something going wrong in their own life. If someone has high emotional energy, their capacity is much higher for acknowledging what's wrong with the situation, thinking of a proper and appropriate solution, and working to carry out that situation.

Someone who has a lot of emotional energy has a higher chance of keeping their emotional energy high, while someone who has very little emotional energy has a much higher chance of staying at a low energy level until someone imparts more positive emotional energy into their personal space.

Mental Energy

Mental energy is that which helps you with reasoning, creativity, and strategy. Someone with a lot of mental energy will read often, they'll like puzzles, they'll be making, building, or creating things, and they'll have a high capacity for reasoning through mental exercises that others might not.

Like with physical energy, the more consistently you make use of the energy you have, the more easily you will be able to create and use mental energy.

Where Does Energy Come From?

With emotional energy, the long and short of it is that emotions themselves are energy. When you think of energy, how much there is, how it works, and how to evaluate how much you have, it's important to note that in each of these categories, there is such a thing as negative energy. This is energy that ruins, detracts from, or even inhibits the energy that you have in each category.

When you're thinking about the source of emotional energy, you will find that there isn't really a limit on how much you can have, unless a limit is in some way imposed by your mental or hormonal health or capabilities. These energy levels can all be drastically affected by your mental and hormonal health, so be sure to speak with your doctor if things aren't improving for you with the use of the techniques laid out in this book.

Mental energy comes from your use of the mental muscles, so to speak. The more you do with the energy you have and the more you keep your mind working, the easier it will be to keep more and more cycling through while you're working on thinking about things, creating things, and so much else that mental energy allows for you to do.

For the most part, the energy that you have is affected and determined by how much you're doing on a regular basis, how you're using the energy that you do have, and what negative energy elements are present in your life. If you're unsure what activities you can do to increase your energy, the best place to start is with the things that are of interest to you.

With mental energy, you could take up things like sudoku, different forms of art, writing, reading, or other activities that are mentally stimulating.

With emotional energy, you could look into things that are emotionally rewarding like volunteer work with people or animals, spending time with family and friends, working on your emotional health, journaling, and things that make you feel emotionally gratified.

With physical energy, take up some activities that will require you to expend physical energy. Start by engaging in activities that don't expend more energy than you have like walking, swimming, ping pong, yoga, or tennis. Since everyone's threshold for physical energy is different, you will need to gauge this and go with things that feel right for you.

Over time, as you do these things, you will find that your capacity for these energies will increase, you will have the ability to think of more and more things that you could be doing with the energy you have and, the more you spend within your limits, the more you will ultimately get back.

You never get back more energy by *overspending* your energies, though. Be aware of your limits, be aware of how much energy you have, and stop overspending it. Be willing to wait a little while to build up the capacity for things that you want to do. The time will pass anyway, and I'll bet you'd rather be better off when it does.

What Can Drain Your Energy?

The biggest cause of energy drainage, aside from people who drain it from you, is overextension. Putting yourself into a position in which you have to give more than you're getting, you will often be overextending. Let's clarify this a little bit more with some examples.

Let's say that you have enough emotional energy to handle some light idle chatter with someone, and then you're going to need to go home and do some things for yourself in order to bring that back.

You might need to take a relaxing bath, write out your emotions in your journal, talk with your significant other, call your mother, and things of this nature.

So, you're in this emotional position and someone calls you to tell you that their boyfriend has just left them, and they need someone to talk to about what's happened. This now requires that you expend more emotional energy than you have. It's one of those things that can't necessarily be avoided in life, as it's not something your friend intended, and it is typical to want to be there for our friends when they need us.

The next day, you will find that you have just a bit less energy to deal with things that come across your path than you did on the day before. It helps to think of energy as some sort of rollover program in which unused energy is added to the following day. Only, in this case, if you overspend, you're spending the next day's energy.

Doing things like this with any consistency can end up putting you behind the eight ball, so to speak. If you are consistently taking from the next day's energy, that total amount of energy will deplete over time and it will get harder and harder to replenish your energy and you will feel like you're constantly fighting to deal with the things that come up from day to day.

These situations can lead us to feel like we're not doing well mentally or emotionally. These can lead us into a darker, more depressing place because we simply cannot handle the things that are happening in our environments from day to day.

Monitoring your emotional health from day to day is so important because if you see a pattern in how you've been feeling, you can more easily isolate where it started, what changes contributed to it, and how to turn things around.

Chapter 3: How to Stop Absorbing Other Peoples' Distress

The Effects of Absorbing Distress

One of the biggest hurdles an empath has to overcome is the fact that they absorb the emotions of the people around them. Passing, encountering, or dealing with someone who is experiencing a lot of emotional distress will affect an empath, as simply being near that emotional output is enough to take it on for themselves, whether they intend to or not. That is until they learn how to control that impulse and that response.

Taking on the distress from others can take a high toll on someone who is highly sensitive to it. If you're unaware of where the feeling is coming from and that it isn't your distress to own, it can seem like depression or like you have no control over your emotional responses to the things going on in your life. Feeling like you have no control, in itself, can be cause for quite a bit of emotional distress.

Before getting a handle on what it feels like to experience the emotional distress of others and before understanding how you should respond to this, it can seem unshakable. It feels like it won't leave you and like nothing you can do will alleviate the problem, but I promise, there is help to be found for this mechanism and you will be able to run it on and off as you wish.

How to Shut it Down

Like with most things in life, the first step to being able to manage it is realizing that it's a problem and what the problem is. The problem is that you're extremely perceptive of the emotional distress being felt around you and that you can't seem to stop taking that distress into yourself. The problem is that someone else's pain is making you feel pain.

So, when you're in a place where you're taking on the pain of another, it can be a result of a couple of different types of situations. One of those is one that you've probably experienced on a number of occasions and which will be a bit more common for you. The most common type of empath is the one who takes on the emotions of the person they're interacting with. So, this would mean you're talking with someone about something that is causing them distress. Your response to this is to go further than wanting to help them, wishing they didn't feel this way, and feeling sad that they're dealing with the things they're dealing with.

This usually feels a little bit like some anxiety, a need to do something about it, and like the situation being described is actually happening to you. It can feel like you can't pull back from it because you feel a sense of duty to be there and help fix it, even if no person or social convention would require that of you.

An empath will be familiar with the strain they feel when they're not able to hop in and fix a problem that someone who is close to them is experiencing. They'll be familiar with what it's like to feel like they cannot say no when someone asks for help, because they know that puts the other person into a bind.

When you Notice you're Absorbing the Distress of Someone you Know

1. Express your concern for their circumstances to the person.
2. Assure the person that you hope for the best for them.
3. Offer help that you can comfortably and safely give.
4. Remove yourself from their immediate area.
5. Close your eyes and focus on your body and your mind. Be mindful and be present.
6. Focus your energy on the things you are trying to accomplish and the things that you are working on currently.

This will take practice and it will feel less effective if the person in question is going through something that is life-changing or exceedingly traumatic. You can do this process and steps five and six until you get a positive result.

This part of being an empath requires practice. Knowing when to pull yourself out of a situation for your own well-being and knowing what you can comfortably handle is a huge part of safeguarding your mental and emotional health. Stay vigilant when helping friends with their struggles and don't allow yourself to take a back seat to others.

The other type of situation is one that occurs with slightly less regularity, but it's not uncommon for empaths. Say you're out in a public place one day when someone nearby is dealing with a heavy emotional burden. The emotional energy that the person is giving off can transfer to you as an empath. You can absorb that energy by being nearby, seeing them dealing with, and you can feel that someone in your surroundings is upset or in distress.

This can make it difficult to get through your day if you end up getting saddled with the feeling that others are having, whether you are feeling that way or not. So, it's important to be able to distance yourself from it when you see it happening.

When you Notice You're Absorbing a Stranger's Distress:

1. Tell yourself that the feelings are not yours.
2. Close your eyes, inhale deeply and exhale through your mouth.

3. Envision yourself breathing in all the bad emotions around you to gather them up, then blowing them away on your exhale to disperse them.
4. Tell yourself that you don't need to feel that emotion and understand that you are not obligated to feel that way.
5. Focus on what you are in that space to accomplish and put all of your energy into getting that thing completed.
6. Allow yourself to leave that dispersed energy behind and move forward, energized in your plans for what you are trying to accomplish.

It can sometimes be easier to pull yourself out of the emotions of strangers than the emotions of the people you know personally. Knowing someone personally gives you some measure of investment in those emotions and it makes you feel like you need to take some amount of responsibility for resolving them, which may or may not be true depending on what caused the emotions and what's going on in life around you.

So, when you get a random emotion that seems like it's out of nowhere and you just make a concentrated effort to push it away from yourself, you will generally get a more positive result, and you will feel more empowered as time goes on. You won't feel like this is something that is anything more than a minor obstacle when you get truly skilled at pushing those emotions away from yourself.

How to Cope in the Meantime

While you're learning how to keep yourself safe from the emotional distress of the people around you, there are several things you can do to help you to cope with the difficulty that you're feeling.

It may come as a surprise to some that the coping mechanisms are so simple for such complex emotions and troubles. This is, however, by design. This is because one is already dealing with so much, we don't want the mechanisms we use to take more energy than the person likely has. We want the person to be able to do just enough to cause a disruption in that negative emotional response, so the more logical part of the mind can take over and interject more positive into the mental process.

Let's take a look at some of the things one can do to turn around the difficulty they're having with the negative emotions of others.

Change What You Can

Spending time lamenting over the things in your situation that you cannot change will often make things worse for you, so it's important to center your focus on the things that you can readily and easily change. You can go to another space, you can change your clothes to something more comfortable, and you can change many small things in your environment that can contribute to perpetuating negative feelings.

If it would make you feel better to be somewhere else, to eat something if you haven't recently, to watch something on television, to journal, or anything else that you're not currently doing, go ahead and make the changes that you can make.

As you continue to flex this muscle, you will find that you're more and more able to make the changes that need to be made to make you feel better. You will find that the list of the things you can change to make a positive impact on you will grow with each time you do it.

Don't underestimate yourself or sell yourself short, but don't take on more than you can handle. This is a very delicate balance when you're starting out, but you will get the hang of it and you will be able to figure out the things you can do without setting yourself back further than you started.

Find an Outlet

This is something you will need to find for yourself, as it is one of those things that will vary from person to person. While getting suggestions from the people around you in life is an ideal way of finding out about new things you can do to help you, don't feel obligated to take those suggestions if they don't quite fit in with what works for you.

Some people like to do very light and relaxing things, while some others prefer to do something a little more arduous and involved.

Common outlets are:

Pottery
Coloring
Writing
Reading
Painting
Woodworking
Organizing
Cleaning
Budgeting
Life planning
Origami
Aromatherapy
Candle making

As you can see, there isn't much of a central theme between each of these options, but there is an element of mental involvement for each of them. This is what you want for this kind of coping mechanism, as something that otherwise engages your mind will help you not to be so consumed by the things that are going on with others around you or others who are in your life.

There aren't any right or wrong answers when it comes to these coping mechanisms **unless** they're harmful to you or another. It's important to be courteous, safe, and legal when you make your choices for coping strategies and outlets.

Tell Yourself it Will Be Okay

This is not a coping strategy that is based on the power of illusion or deception. This is you telling yourself the truth and getting yourself to understand this on a very basic level. When you are feeling intense negative emotion that isn't yours, you will be okay at the end of it. There is nothing in your life that is causing you to feel these emotions, so there isn't anything to fix. There is nothing you've done incorrectly or that you've done to deserve these feelings, and you will feel better before too long. *It will be okay.*

Write it Out

Writing out how you're feeling when you end up taking on the emotions of people around you can be helpful in two ways. In the first way, it can help you to get all of those emotions out of you and onto the page. The value of this really cannot be overstated, and it's a shame that as few people see the value that exists in it. When you're dealing with emotions internally and you're not talking about them with people, there are quite a few things that you might never even know about those emotions or about how you really feel.

When you're forced to elaborate on your emotions or to explain them to others, you will go through more of the deeper things that contribute to making the emotions as intense as they are for you. You will find out why things hit you in the way that they do, and you might even find that you could relate this emotion to other emotional responses that you've had in other areas of your life. This is an important piece of the puzzle in your mind.

The second way in which this can be helpful is that it can provide you with a record. As you work on lessening the impact of the emotions of others on your personal life and yourself, you can get some very valuable information by reading through what you've written.

By looking through that record of your emotions and the impact you've been experiencing over time, you can tell if your strategies are really working. You can see the progress where you may not otherwise be able to see it.

Progress is such an important part of mental health, as your health is not a switch with "good" and "bad" functions.

Improving your mental health is a constant effort and it's something that needs to be maintained over your entire life and it's something that is far more important than a good deal of us seem to realize.

Get a good amount of sleep

This can be somewhat of a hot-button issue for some. If you're having difficulty with insomnia or if you tend to oversleep and feel worse as a result of it, you might want to talk with your doctor about figuring out how to find a middle ground that works for you.

For some, taking melatonin before bed will help them drift off to sleep more easily and to stay there without too much hassle. For some, drinking tea or meditating does more for them to improve this effort.

For those who oversleep, getting a good amount of sleep would mean having to cut down. In such cases, finding things to do in the evenings and in the mornings that are stimulating, enjoyable, and worthwhile can be a good way to keep yourself from sleeping through all the time you have between working shifts.

Those who have experienced clinical depression may be familiar with this pattern of coming home from work, watching some television, not eating a proper meal, then sleeping until it's time to go back to work, repeating this cycle day after day. This is both a symptom and perpetuation of depression and should be talked about with your doctor if you spot such a pattern in your own life.

Chapter 4: Protecting Yourself from Narcissists and Energy Vampires

What is a Narcissist?

A narcissist is a person who has a low threshold for empathy, who seeks gratification from vain means or who seeks egotistical admiration of their own idealized self-image. This means that they're looking for people who will admire them, they admire themselves, and that a good deal of their attention is spent on ensuring that the way they come across to others is as perfect as possible. There is a vital need and drive to look and be perfect when others can see them and there is a compulsion to receive praise and validation from others.

There is a fairly important distinction between being narcissistic and being self-centered. Self-centered or self-serving people will often do things that are to their own benefit before the benefit of others, but they are rarely malicious and rarely are they unresponsive to empathy or pleas for compassion. There are many traits of the narcissist that will set them apart from others you will encounter, and their behaviors are generally quite toxic. Being around a narcissistic person for too long will generally have ill effects on people of positive intent or character.

Finding out what a narcissist's intentions and motivations are can be difficult, but at the center of everything will be gratification for them. It will be something that gains them positive attention, envy of them, or positive feedback about the person and their accomplishments. Narcissists will often say things like, "Love me or hate me, you can't deny that I'm here," or "It doesn't matter what people are saying about you; just that they're talking about you."

Narcissism itself is a personality disorder that is characterized by needing to be seen, needing to be the center of attention, and needing to be seen as involved in things at the center of attention. Narcissism can manifest in many ways, and it can be more insidious than people may initially realize or give it credit for. Narcissism can drive others to do things like sabotage others or cause issues to meet their own needs.

The term narcissism is derived from the story of Narcissus in Greek mythology, who fell in love with his own reflection in a pool. Depending on your familiarity with Greek mythology, you might be able to make a pretty accurate guess at the outcome of this particular tale. Let's just say that things didn't quite go his way.

Being so concerned with yourself, your own image, and what you want in life that you have little to no regard for the suffering or detriment of the people around you is something that is, in itself, a pretty big issue. That being said, it can also lead to a good number of other problems for the narcissist and for the people who are connected to or closely invested in them.

Given what we've detailed in this chapter and in the last, you can see pretty clearly that the differences between empaths and narcissists are pretty stark. Some might go so far as to call them two ends of a spectrum when it comes to empathy, decency, and regard for others.

The unfortunate thing is that in spite of the personalities and the concerns of the narcissist and the empath being so greatly polarized, this fact doesn't always keep the two from making a connection in life. The narcissist will often think of people in terms of their usefulness and will see people in terms of the things they have to offer them. In such a case, a narcissist will see an empath as a person they can use to meet their own needs in life.

While the energy vampire and the narcissist both have the capacity to drain energy from people, particularly from empaths, there are some key differences that we'll explore in the next chapter.

There is a great deal of energy and usefulness to be found in the empath by people like narcissists and energy vampires, so it's important to stay aware of who these people are, what they want, and how to avoid them.

How to Recognize a Narcissist

A narcissist will, in some cases, work to conceal their behaviors. In a good number of cases, however, the behaviors can be spotted if you know what to look for. If you can find several of the typical traits of a narcissist within someone you know, then you would do well to put some distance between you.

Narcissists, due to their callous nature and motivation, will generally be very poor friends. People who always seem to need something without ever really being there to return the favor. The traits they exhibit with the people who are closest to them would put some emotional pressure on people with even the strongest constitutions and the thickest skin. Narcissistic behavior isn't generally something that should be tolerated.

For an empath, however, being involved with a narcissist can have catastrophic consequences. Empaths tend to throw themselves into their relationships with others and tend to give very much for those relationships. For someone who will generally take as much as they can take from someone closest to them, an empath is a gift. For the empath, it can be draining and nearly deadly when dealing with having to give more than they possess, dealing with criticisms that narcissists generally lay on the people closest to them, and having to deal with the negative emotions that the narcissist will experience from day to day.

Take a look at the section below and see if you know anyone who shows these traits or fits these descriptions. If so, then you might be dealing with someone with narcissistic tendencies. If you know someone who exhibits more than seven of the traits below, you would do well to pull back from that person as early as is possible.

The Traits of the Narcissist

1. Envy is a huge focus of theirs, and they assume that everyone is envious of them.

   Much of what the narcissist says will be centered around whether or not someone else has something that the narcissist does not. They will be overly concerned about how much someone else has, what they did to deserve that, how the narcissist can get it, and how it makes the narcissist look that the other person has something while the narcissist does not.

   To those who know the narcissist, this will be the subject of discussion when they see a thing or a situation that someone has when they do not. There will be a nearly obsessive need to return to that subject matter if it is not properly addressed and the narcissist will feel the need to find a way in which they are better than or more superior than that person.

2. They do not or cannot respect the boundaries of others.

    The narcissist doesn't particularly care what boundaries are set by the people around them. They will acknowledge those boundaries if they are forced to do so but will generally come up with some excuse as to why that boundary can't or should not apply to them. These excuses are often nonsensical or flimsy at their best.

    Boundaries are important in any friendship. Your friends should not be asking questions that make you uncomfortable, your friends should not be overstaying their welcome in your home, your friends should not be coming over at odd hours of the night for no reason unless you've discussed and agreed upon the acceptability of such behaviors.

    Attempts to ask a narcissist to respect your boundaries will often be met with some statement of offense at the notion or some incredulity that you would feel the need to insist. This could also invite such unpleasant things as tantrums, guilt trips, accusations, backhanded comments, or uncouth suggestions about your character and why you would need such boundaries.

3. They believe themselves to be superior to others.

   As partially addressed in item one, the narcissist will often think of themselves as being higher above others. They'll see themselves as "being cut from better cloth," as more deserving of positive things, and generally just as better as other people. They don't particularly have much basis for thinking this aside from statements like, "Look at me," or other such vague statements.

   Attempts to remind the narcissist to be humble will often push the narcissist into more defensive territory, wherein they'll start to lash out, say hurtful things, or make unfair suggestions about the shortcomings of people around them.

4. They are not effective communicators.

   Communicating with another person requires that you relate to them on some level. It required that you see things from one another's point of view, it requires that you don't condescend to the person in front of you, and it requires a willingness to hear and understand someone else.

   Narcissists will often be invested solely in the contributions they have to make to a conversation. They will often find themselves to be the most interesting people in the conversation and won't see much cause for getting any feedback on what they've said.

The above is an extreme case, but you will often find that a narcissist doesn't particularly hear what you've said because they just kind of "check out" after they've finished talking.

5. They are a perfectionist in a way that demands the people around them be perfect as well.

The narcissist has a need to be seen as perfect on some level. They will often "give advice," that comes across more as an insult on who you are, what you look like, how you respond to things, and they will often imply that those who are not as callous as they are, are simply weak.

They will insist that the people who are married to them, who live with them, work with them, are related to them in any way are kept to a certain standard, or are written off or regarded as less valid.

6. They tend to exaggerate their abilities.

The narcissist wants everyone to know that they are the ones for the job. They want people to know what others have said about them, they want others to know what they have done that sets them apart from others. Another notable fact about this is that the narcissist will usually fabricate most of those facts. They want you to know that they are the leader in something, whether or not there is any factual basis for that.

7. Attempts to get them to take responsibility for their actions result in blaming others and deflection.

The narcissist will deflect anything they can, and they will generally utilize negative emotion as their means of doing it. They will blame others for reasons they couldn't do something, they will bring up negative things about others that have nothing to do with the situation at hand to get you to stop asking them about their own shortcomings, and sometimes they will feign some sort of emotional breakdown in order to change the subject to one that gets them more attention and sympathy.

8. They are typically obsessed with success and creating an image of success for all to see.

This trait fits in with the fifth item on this list. They typically want to put forward an image of success, accomplishment, affluence, and it doesn't generally matter very much if they are in debt, if they are not doing very well financially, or if they've sustained a lot of failures.

These things do not make the narcissist feel like they're not a complete success. The narcissist's need for the image of success will keep them in the habit of telling others that they have had nothing but success.

This is like the extreme version of "saving face," but they do it when no one asks.

9. They have an overblown or an inflated sense of their own importance.

The narcissist will often assume that they are an essential part of a project, group, company, job, or effort. This assumption and insistence are usually based on nothing but their own gut feeling and their own need to be in the middle of things and to be praised for their success.

In friendship, a narcissist might talk about assisting to pull off a party or group event when they had very little to do with it. The simple act of making a suggestion for where to have the event will give the narcissist the impression that, without them, the event would have been utterly impossible.

10. They thrive on having control of the situation and of others.

Being in control of the situation and the people in it is the perfect place for the narcissist to ensure that things are going their way and that everyone is aware that the narcissist is in charge. The narcissist will generally take positions of leadership as lightly as possible in terms of their physical commitment and contribution to the job.

Question the involvement of the narcissist in a project in which they were "in charge," however, and you will be informed that the narcissist was present at every phase of the project, oversaw every aspect of the project, and was instrumental in every decision that was made in order to complete it.

11. They tend to be overly sensitive about their imperfections.

Bringing up the imperfections or shortcomings of a narcissist will result in an immediate verbal attack. The narcissist will come back at you with vicious insults or suggestions about your character, and they will not be reasoned with when people voice concern about these outbursts.

This is the type of thing that will usually be followed up with an insistence on an apology to the narcissist for "attacking their character," or something as severe as this. Any suggestions that the narcissist should improve or might not be perfect will be met with vitriol, vigor, and an incongruously negative response.

12. Their personal relationships are typically a mess.

As you might suggest, someone who is close to a narcissist will not stay in that position for very long. Those who do will often have methods for dealing with those people which will mitigate the toxicity of their responses to certain things.

They will say things like, "There are just certain things I never bring up to them, and I'll change the subject if they bring it up," and "Oh, they're fine if you just avoid certain topics." This is a survival mechanism that people devise in order to stay connected to people who have toxic traits, without succumbing to that toxicity.

13. They expect special treatment in most circumstances.

Because of their perceived superiority, importance, and influence, the narcissist will often believe that there are some exceptions to be made for them. There are things that should be considered for them that would not be considered for the people around them or for other people in their position.

If you ask such a person why they feel they deserve such treatment, they will respond by saying that they simply think they deserve it, that they deserve the best, or that they're not even asking very much.

This is semi-connected to their disrespect for boundaries as well.

14. They typically come across as arrogant.

Given all the examples that have been given about narcissistic behavior in the above items, I think you can see the inherent arrogance in those traits. There are very few of these traits that someone can exhibit without coming across as exceedingly arrogant. Their belief in their pedigree, their superiority, and their disregard for manners or social convention hint at a very high level of arrogance in that person.

15. Criticism is met with extreme anger.

This is a much more intense display than this state in item number eleven. The narcissist will respond to criticism of their actions, assumptions, computations, and their character in such a way that is completely incongruous to the criticism sustained.

The narcissist will sometimes "vow to destroy" someone who "humiliates" them by suggesting that they might not be correct or infallible.

16. They feel as though they are owed or entitled to things.

The narcissist will generally feel an entitlement to things that are not available to others. They'll feel that they deserve handouts, opportunities, possessions, and more simply because of who they are.

The narcissist will often have difficulty finding something they don't feel they deserve because of who they are.

17. A deep sense of insecurity hides under their façade.

The narcissist will let slip on very rare occasions that they are not nearly as secure as they make themselves seem. Their tendencies to lash out at the simplest embarrassment or at the simplest criticism shows that they have a lot to hide under the lies that they insist the people around them believe.

18. They tend to take advantage of the people around them.

The narcissist will often think of people in terms of what they can get from them. The more value they see in a particular person, the closer they will keep them because they have a higher capacity for usefulness than others. Because of this, they will often take far more than they will give.

19. Empathy doesn't come very easily—if at all—to them.

Narcissism exists somewhere on the spectrum between empathetic person and psychopathy in terms of the threshold for empathy that exists within the condition.

This is usually something you can spot by how the narcissist responds to people who are in a lower income bracket, or who are having a difficult time. If they make no accommodations for such people, they typically have much lower empathy.

Such things would look like leaving no tip in a restaurant and telling the server that if they wanted more money, they should have chosen a different job. This would look like a professor insisting that a student turns in a large homework assignment in spite of a death in the family because "that's really not my problem."

These are displays of a lack of empathy and should be seen as a red flag in the people that we keep closest to us.

20. They believe that they are unique or special in a way that makes them better than the people around them.

There is often some inarticulable quality that the narcissist believes they have which makes them more valuable, more desirable, and generally better than other people who might be in the same position as they. This is generally not backed up by any fact they can provide, and they will generally respond badly—if at all—to questions about why this is.

21. If they don't receive copious compliments, admiration, adoration, and effusive praise, they will take it badly.

The narcissist will often make very obvious bids for your attention, ask for you to pay them compliments, and will become very visibly upset if their obvious attempts at garnering flattery go unnoticed or unheeded.

Most such situations will be met with anger, contempt, or even suggestions that you don't care about this. This is a manipulation tactic.

22. They will see very small contributions on their part as much larger than they are.

If a narcissist has to impart any sort of contribution to some project or effort of any kind, they will typically overblow that contribution until it sounds like they've given everything they have and more to make that thing happen.

Let's say you've helped a narcissist move to a new house. You've picked up the moving truck, you've helped get the truck loaded, you've driven it to the new house, you've overseen getting it unloaded, you've returned the truck and picked up the difference in the deposit as a housewarming gift, and you even stayed to help them get settled in for the night.

The narcissist will see buying pizza for dinner (which they shared with you) as being exceedingly generous and as the greatest contribution for the entire affair. Even if they picked a different pizza place than anyone asked for!

What is an Energy Vampire?

Positive energies that are exuded by the people around you can be rejuvenating. It's that part about a person that makes them "refreshing to be around," and it's that aspect of them that makes spending time with them more relaxing than tiring. People who are introverted and who don't enjoy spending time with many people will often bond with one person who produces and exudes positive energy, and they will prefer to spend their time with that person because they don't exhaust them.

While these people who generate positive energy are people to be valued and appreciated, they are also people who need to be protected. This is because people who exude that positive energy is a lot like magnets. The positive will attract the negative. That positive energy isn't just useful to people who are generally positive; it's useful to anyone who encounters it and it can help people, no matter what their intentions are with other people.

In addition to this, there is a polar opposite of the energy vampire. The energy vampire exudes a negative energy that pulls the positive right out of you. They are exhausting people to be around, and they know how exhausting they are to be around. The energy that people lose around people who drain it from you will, in some small measure, go right to the vampire.

This is where the vampire title is more appropriate than "energy dissipator." They do get some benefit of sapping the energy out of you, but it's not very much and it's not enough to sustain them for very long. This generally means that energy vampires will continue to appear in the life of someone who exudes positive energy in order to get what small benefits they can.

Energy vampires will also tend to pick up on the actions of theirs that cause a rush of positive energy out of you, and they will focus on doing those frequently because they're interested in drawing that positive energy from you. Positive energy is something that most people need in order to survive and to be happy. Positive energy is what gets us through the day, it's what allows us to get through the worst parts of the day, and it gives us the strength to deal with things that come from various negative things in life.

Another thing to note about energy vampires is that their behaviors aren't limited to one specific personality type. Their unique dispositions, when paired with their innate energy-draining properties make for a few different personality types that you may recognize.

The Victim

This person does enough whining about the status quo, the things that have been done or said in their vicinity, the things that have been done or said to them, and the things that adversely affect them, whether they're closely involved or not. This person will never be looking for solutions but will always have something to say about how bad things are going.

The Melodramatic

This person is sometimes known as the Drama Queen, as they always seem to be able to put themselves right at the center of anything that is going wrong, any conflicts that come from silly sources. This type of person will often talk about hating being involved in drama, but when suggestions are made to keep them from getting involved, they will never make an effort to take them and will make excuses for why they need to continue dealing with, perpetuating, and causing trouble.

The Passive-Aggressive

This is the type of person who will tell you that nothing is wrong when you ask but will tell others that you've done something to horribly offend them. These people are not the type to ever be direct about how they feel about things that are going on as they're happening. They're not one to cause conflict by telling someone directly that they have an issue and would like to resolve it. They thrive on creating conflict that gets people talking and which presents very little risk to them. If they don't say these hurtful or rude things in front of you, you can't get mad at them and make them take responsibility for their actions.

The Irascible

This is the person who always seems to need to "vent" about things that make them very angry. This person seems to sweep into your life with a wave of anger and negative energy, then will do nothing to attempt to remove that energy or improve the vibe of the space. There are often legitimate reasons for this person to be angry, but they seem to have more reasons to be angry than anyone else in your life and they seem to have reason to be angry more often than they have reasons to be happy.

If an energy vampire knows they can count on you as a source of positive energy, then they will keep coming around you, they will keep doing the things they know leech the most positive energy from you, and they will be interested in creating as many opportunities to do that as possible.

This is where the danger is in having an energy vampire in your life; they will be looking for ways to ensure they have more time with you and more time in which to leech energy from you. If you realize that someone is an energy vampire, you would do well to remove them from your life as quickly as possible and be aware of their attempts to interject themselves into more areas of your life.

How to Spot Energy Drainers

When you're trying to spot people, who seek to leech positive energy from you, you need to be vigilant. A lot of the behaviors above can be noticed over an extended period of time, thanks to the fact that their behaviors are a pattern. However, letting an emotional vampire into your life for long enough that they can establish such a pattern can be harmful to you. You will spend more time having your positive energy taken from you, and you risk becoming more connected with the person and you risk disconnection or mitigated connection being more difficult.

When you meet someone who you suspect is an energy vampire, your best course of action is to clam up a little bit when you first meet them. If you get the vibe, through your empathic means, that this person can and will suck positive energy from you, do your best to keep to yourself when they're around and do your best not to show that the positive energy in the environment is coming from you. Keep to the people you know and talk quietly. Enjoy yourself but try to fade into the backdrop a little bit.

You will generally know energy drainers and vampires by the reputation that precedes them. Those who know them will tend to feel like the person is more negative than positive. It can also help to let your existing circle of friends know that you don't do well when spending time with people who exhibit the most notable traits of energy vampires. This way, if they happen to know someone like that, they will be more inclined to warn you upfront or to make efforts to keep you separated from that person on occasions when you happen to be in the same vicinity.

How to Keep Energy Drainers at Bay

Attempts made by energy vampires to get closer to you should be met with disinterested or half-hearted attempts to commit to time spent together. Making excuses for why you can't spend time getting to know someone who you know has these traits, is a great way to keep them from getting too close. There is nothing wrong with being courteous about your declinations for spending time with them, but you should do your best to keep yourself from being too available to people with these tendencies and traits.

If the person seems to be bent on making a connection with you, being in the places where you are, doing things to bring themselves closer to you, then you can make it clear that you just don't have the time to get involved in anything at the moment and that it would be unfair for you to try to make plans with someone when you've been struggling to fit your other friends and family into what little free time you do have. Being busy is a very typical thing for people these days and is generally understood when it's brought up.

If this is someone who is intimately connected with your circle of friends and family, then you would do well to talk about it with others in your circle who can be discreet. Simply let them know that the person has some traits that make you uncomfortable, that spending time with that person isn't something you're interested in doing for long periods of time if it can be avoided. Generally, when asked about something like this, friends and family can "run interference" for you and help to keep a degree of separation between you.

Making your intentions clear to people you don't want to spend time with is generally the best way to go. As they say, honesty is the best policy. That being said, it can often be less comfortable to tell someone that you don't wish to spend time with them, and negative people can react unpredictably when they're refused something that they want. Amongst mature adults, you're less likely to find someone who will pitch a fit when someone says they don't want to be around them, but there are exceptions to this rule.

Chapter 5: Empaths, Parenting & Sensitive Children

Children with High Emotional Sensitivity

One of the main difficulties one will face with children who are empathic is that the emotional health of a child may be a little bit harder to navigate than that of an adult. A child can't tell you, right off the bat, why they feel the way they do if someone else is responsible for how they feel, where the emotion is coming from, and how they're really feeling. Generally, you will find that a child will tell you whether they're feeling "good" or they're feeling "bad."

This, unfortunately, really doesn't give you a lot to go on when trying to assess what your child is dealing with, where it's coming from, and how best to help them cope. There are some signs you can look for, though, that can help you to determine if your child is empathic or highly sensitive.

They Are Receptive to the Energies Around Them

This will generally manifest in their asking what's wrong when you've said nothing to give them the impression that anything is wrong, and it can also result in their feeling like other kids are mad at them in school when no one has said anything rude to them.

They Are More Sensitive to Stimuli Than Other Children

Highly sensitive children will often cry when others cry, will be startled very easily, exceedingly ticklish, laugh when others laugh, or they might even go into sensory overload before other children might.

This is something that has come to be an indication of children who are on the autism spectrum, but it's not something that is exclusive to that. People who are sensitive to the things in their environment can experience everything going on around them, all at once. When this happens, the person will often feel the need to flee the area, cover their ears, close their eyes, or they might scream.

A child who is feeling sensory overload might feel like they're under attack by the area around them and all of the things going on in it. This can be scary when it happens, but even breathing, a quiet area, and cool temperatures can help the person to feel like things are starting to normalize.

They Cry When Other Children Do, or They Cry When People Get Angry

Children who are very sensitive to the emotions of others will often mirror them. They are not aware that the emotion is theirs and they're still in the phase of life where they will say how they feel, or they will show it if they don't know how to say what they're feeling.

Instances of this are most apparent when the child is fine, playing, happy, and doing well until another child in the area gets upset or hurt. The child might immediately begin crying, despite nothing being wrong for them personally.

Their Feelings Stick with Them

Some children, after a reprimand, will go right back to playing after a brief period of sadness. An empathic child, however, will often find themselves thinking about being yelled at for a much longer period of time. These periods will grow longer and longer as their attention spans mature and grow.

It is generally much harder for someone who is highly sensitive to move past a feeling of intense negative energy, so be mindful of this when you lose your temper. Do your best to apologize when you do so unjustly and be sure to level with the child about the things they're feeling. Let them feel like they can talk to you about the way you make them feel, without fear of repercussion.

Animals Seem Drawn to and Comfortable with Them

Children who are very in tune with their emotions are typically the children that animals will instinctively trust and want to protect. Because of this, you might notice your cat nudging its head against the baby's, the dog laying by the crib or bed, or even the bird mimicking the things the baby says.

You may also notice the animals beginning to respond when the child is upset. Staying closer when the child is sad or mad, laying in their bed when they are sick, or even watching over them until they fall asleep.

They Think More Than Other Children Their Age

Highly sensitive people tend to be very pensive and tend to think about the larger questions in life. They tend to wonder why things work the way they do, why the more minute details of human behavior are the way they are, and why people tend to follow certain patterns.

As young children, however, these types of things are harder to articulate, and you might find that your child asks *fewer* questions as a result. While they're deeply inquisitive in their

84

minds, they may reserve their questions for when they feel they can properly state them to ensure they get a good answer.

Asking your children what they're thinking about, however, can give them the forum to try to work out what they mean with you. You can help them to figure out what it is they want to know, then you can answer those questions for them. This helps your connection with them immensely and will solidify your position with them as a source of helpful information and as someone who can help them to eliminate confusion.

Displays of Their Compassion Are Not Limited to the Living

A child who is highly sensitive or empathic might find that they feel guilty about being rude to a teddy bear. They have an intrinsic understanding of how emotions feel (even if they don't know why they feel that way, where they come from, or how to articulate those feelings), and they know that they don't want to feel certain feelings.

This can make it much harder for an empath to want to throw away dolls, toys, drawings, and books. They can tend to assign personalities and feelings to these things and they will tell you if they feel bad about putting them in positions that would be disagreeable for a person in those same positions.

This can be frustrating for moms who want to clear the way for new toys or to have a yard sale, but through creativity, you can generally help the child to understand that the place the toys are going will be better for the toys, better for the child, better for you, and better for the house.

Things on TV Affect Them to a Large Degree

Children who are highly sensitive will cry during sad movies, they'll scream about bad things happening to characters on screen, and those feelings might not go away for a while. Watching a movie where bad things happen to the cute little character they like, whether the situation gets resolved or not, could be quite the emotional ordeal for the young empath.

Movies or shows with strong emotional content should be watched when the child is well-rested. If they are sleepy, these emotions are likely to hit them much harder and more loudly.

They Enjoy Time Spent Alone

Many children are vivacious, outgoing, chatty little people who love to spend time with as many people as they possibly can. The empathic child may be all of these things but may also prefer to spend time on their own when they're permitted to do so. They might like solitary activities like puzzles, coloring, picture books, and more.

This is a recuperative period for the emotional energy the empath needs to spend on being around other people. Each empath is different and may derive a good deal of emotional energy from being extroverted. The empath, however, will also find that their emotional energy is spent by absorbing the emotions and the sensations in the world around them.

Time to oneself and time spent being quiet and still is very recuperative and healthy for the empath, so not to worry! Just bear in mind that there is a proper balance for everything.

They Know When You're Lying to Them

This ability isn't just limited to you; they can often tell if another child isn't being truthful with them and they're not generally very gullible. Certain things that we want to tell our children like Santa Claus, the Tooth Fairy, and other fun lies can often be questioned to a much harsher extent than other children might do.

In addition to this, they know when you're telling them that things are fine if they are not fine. If you and your spouse have gotten into a spat and decide to keep things quiet while the children are present, the empathic child may ask what's wrong and press the issue when you don't answer truthfully.

This is not to say that you owe it to your child to tell them the harsh truth at all times. This is to say, however, that you are going to need to get good at answering questions in an evasive way, and you're going to have to get very skilled at misdirection.

Getting the child interested in something else instead of answering the question is a classic technique that many parents use to an excellent result when their children ask questions to which they don't need the answers at such a stage in their lives.

How to Help Children Cope

Bedtime Meditations

The usefulness of meditation for people does not start at any specific age. People of all ages can benefit from taking quiet moments, clearing their minds, relaxing, and making a comfortable mental space in which they can decompress, recuperate from the day, and make their way into a very relaxed and recuperative sleep.

Bedtime meditations are guided by the parents and can be done while the child lies down, all tucked in and ready for dreams. Simply sit on the edge of the bed and instruct them in closing their eyes, then guide their thought process through the meditation and end off with the child envisioning themselves drifting off to sleep.

You can find specific guides for these meditations from numerous sources online and in bookstores, so if you wouldn't like to come up with them yourself, there is still a wealth of options for you.

This helps with bedtime as a whole, as it offers parent and child some time together, it helps you to bond, and it makes bedtime a much more relaxed and controlled affair without all the fuss that bedtime can sometimes have.

Mindfulness

Mindfulness, when taught from a young age, can help a person to know when and how to detach themselves from the feelings they have had earlier. It helps to bring them into the here and now, and it gives them more even ground from which they can look at what is going on, what they need to do, and it can help them to make increasingly more appropriate and logistically beneficial moves as they grow.

Scheduled Decompression

If you put the time in your child's schedule to come away from the digital screens, to turn off external noise, and to enjoy their own time with themselves, it won't be such a shock each night to remove these things from their environment.

In addition to this, you'll be providing an environment in which being by themselves if recuperative and enjoyable. The child is less likely to end up feeling isolated, abandoned, or frightened in times when there aren't numerous outside distractions keeping them from engaging in their own mind.

Scientific studies tell us as well that removing digital screens from our field of view for a minimum of 30 minutes before bed each night can improve the quality of the sleep we get and the time it takes us to drift off each night.

Five Senses Meditation

This is a skill that you can teach your child to help them to cope when there isn't an adult present to help even them out. If your child is in daycare or school outside of the home, this can be an excellent coping skill to help them continue through their day with much less difficulty.

The principle behind five senses meditation is for the child to focus on their senses when they're feeling an intense rush of negative emotion. Teach them to sit still for a moment, close their eyes, breathe in deeply, and focus on the things around them that they can hear, feel, smell, taste, and then have them open their eyes to look around and focus on what they can see right in front of them.

Doing this puts all of their focus on things that have nothing to do with that negative emotion, gives them the chance to see that nothing around them is physically wrong and that they can relax and solve the problem if it's still an issue.

This will take time for them to learn, but it's an invaluable skill.

Help Them to Choose an Outlet

Things that a child can do when they're feeling upset will help them to relax is very important. This could mean something that they need to do at the moment like the five senses meditation, or this could be something they do each night when they come home, like coloring or playing with blocks.

Whatever your child needs to help get things out should be the focus of this coping strategy. The average child should spend a good deal of their time doing things that bring them joy, as well as doing things that help the family.

Helping with chores from a young age will help them get used to those tasks and it helps the child to feel invested in the wellbeing and the overall operation of the household. Teach them how to set the table, do the dishes, take the trash out, or fold the laundry and set up specific times when they can do these things.

If your child can see these things as therapeutic, they're less likely to allow a hard day to keep them from doing the things they need to do as adults to keep their life on the right track!

Encourage Them to Spend Time by Themselves When They Need It

Make sure your child knows that the time they like to spend with themselves is beneficial. Make sure they're aware that there are no hard feelings if they would rather spend some time doing something in their room by themselves than to watch a movie with the family.

Be understanding of the time they need to themselves and make sure that they feel good about telling you when they need it.

Parenting as an Empath

Parenting as an empath can be quite difficult, as you are acutely aware of the emotions your child is feeling at all times, and you're acutely aware of everyone else's as well. Thanks to this, it can be hard to focus on the things that you need to do throughout the day and in your parenting duties.

It can be hard, when you're feeling the emotions from someone else, not to exhibit those with your child. It can be hard not to respond to your child with the anger that they're personally feeling. It can be hard not to feel the emotions your child is feeling and to take that out on your significant other.

As a result of these things, it's imperative that you take care of yourself and to make time for yourself. You must make sure that you're letting go of the emotions that aren't yours, that you're getting time for yourself to recharge your batteries, that you're not overspending your emotional energy, and that you're doing things that will give you more emotional energy in the following day.

This can mean leaning on your partner from time to time and getting time for yourself when you need it, it can mean an early bedtime for the kids one or two nights per week, it can mean asking a family member or friend to take the kids a couple times per month, or some other escape or release.

Don't allow yourself to get so snowed under all the emotions of the people in your life that you miss out on the opportunities to take care of yourself.

Coping Strategies for the Empathic Parent

Meditation

Meditation has a large number of variations, types, and focuses. It's possible that one type of meditation does nothing for you while another type does everything for you, so be sure to look around. Find a method that works for you and take time to let go of the things in your day that has the potential to keep you from getting the rest you need for the next day.

Mindfulness

Mindfulness can be done mentally, but it can also be done on paper. If you like the concept of mindfulness, and you like the concept of writing down your feelings, try writing your mindfulness thought processes in a journal.

This provides a record of how you're feeling from day to day, and it will also tell you if you're consistently getting a good result from your meditation.

Journaling

Journaling has so many different aspects to it that can be helpful for someone who is dealing with a lot of emotions throughout each day. As an empath with children, you will find that each day has more emotional content than you may have previously experienced before children.

Writing down the way you have been feeling, the way your kids have been feeling, and how your day went can help you to see the things that were done incorrectly, and it can also give you a chance to validate the things you did right.

Too few parents are given the opportunity to validate them for the things they do right with their children and are left feeling like the world's worst parent on those really tough days. I promise you that you're not the world's worst anything and that you're doing great as a parent.

Being a mom or a dad is far more work than anyone without kids would ever understand, and the sheer output of emotional energy throughout each day is staggering. You're doing amazingly and you deserve to validate yourself for the things that go right.

Spend Time with Friends Your Age

Parenting has so many rewards and spending time with your children is such a gift. Spending *all* of your time with your children will turn your poor brain into oatmeal. You need to associate with other adults, to talk about your day, to joke about things, and to watch television that isn't intended for audiences of ten or younger.

Being isolated and having time for yourself is nice for the empath, in proper measure. Balance is important and spending all your time isolated from your friends can make for a bad emotional state. Chances are also that your friends miss you and would like to spend more time with you than they currently are. Like everything in life, this can be hard to schedule. *Especially with children* in your life. However, finding a sitter, having your spouse take over for the evening, or having a friend or family member host them for the evening are options for allowing you to spend some time with your friends.

Even if you're only able to do this one weeknight a month, a few hours with your friends here and there will do more positive things for you than you're giving it credit for right now. I can tell that you're making excuses for why it might not work out to schedule something, but I'm not backing down. Find one evening in the next two weeks that you can spend with your friends and commit to it. Call them right now; I'll wait here.

Find a Creative Outlet

Our creative pursuits can take a backseat when we have children. If this was the case for you, schedule some time when you can go pick that back up, get back into it, and then commit to come regular schedule (it doesn't matter how sparse) on which you can do things with that outlet.

If you don't have such a thing, think of something you would like to do! Think of something you've been meaning to try, something you've wanted to get into, something a friend has been doing and which they could probably show you how to do, or something that just sounds interesting to you. Once you find the thing you'd like to do, schedule a time to get started.

Every new habit starts with the first step toward doing it once.

Chapter 6: Empaths & Work

Disadvantages of High Sensitivity in the Workplace

Being highly sensitive to the stress of others, their anxiety, their anger, and their other negative emotions can make it difficult to focus on the things in your work that you would like to get done! If you have a boss who is going through some difficulty with their boss, you might feel the effects of that stress and anxiety before your boss ever comes to talk to you about it.

The reason this could be disadvantageous is that it can cause a considerable amount of stress for you personally to know that someone else isn't doing well. Especially if you know that the person who is feeling stressed is about to come and give you orders that you have to follow.

There is a saying in the workplace about unpleasant things traveling in a downward trajectory on the corporate ladder, and there is a good deal of truth to it. If someone's boss was angry or rude with them, they will generally pass that negativity downward to the people who are working for them.

Knowing that this is coming your way doesn't necessarily soften the blow. Knowing that someone who isn't even in your department is feeling terrible and then feeling terrible as a result could also cause you a good deal of difficulty in simply trying to make it through your day and to deliver your best work possible to the company that you work for!

Advantages of High Sensitivity in the Workplace

If you have people working under you, it can be incredibly helpful to know when they're not doing well. It can help to know what someone can handle before you even give them the work, and it can help to know exactly what kind of attitude you will get back from the person who works under you before you even bring things to them.

Certain people who are not overly concerned with social decorum, people who are energy vampires, or people who are narcissistic might be more combative, manipulative, or troublesome than someone who simply wants to be there and do their job for you. You, being someone with empathic abilities, can pick up on this type of personality, can pick up on this method of behavior, and can know that you will have to deal with it before it's ever thrown at you.

Having to work with people who are energy vampires or who are narcissistic have their own pitfalls, but as someone who can see that type of personality for what they are, you can protect yourself before they ever get the chance to cause you any trouble.

Being able to understand how the emotions of others work, you are also far more capable of reasoning with customers who are upset, you're far more capable of connecting with the people who you have to work within your day to day, and you're more able to tell how best to relay certain things to the people you need to work within the daily operations of your business.

Ideal Careers for Empaths

These are careers that make hefty usage of the bedside manner, understanding of emotions, personal connection, and the caring attitude that can come from an empath. When you feel the passion for the things that you do, when you know how the people you're caring for are feeling, when you're as invested in the success of the people you're working to help as they are, you will have great success in each of these careers.

Nurse
Psychologist
Life coach
Writer
Veterinarian

Musician

Guidance counselor

Teacher

Social worker

Difficult Careers for Empaths

These are careers that thrive on pressure, occlusion, tenacity, and are centered around some of the darker components of human nature. These are careers that could be very difficult, if not severely damaging to someone with empathic abilities.

Try to think of how it would feel to be in these careers, what the hardest parts of each of these careers are, and how it would feel for you to be the person to have to lead the way in each of those situations; could you do it?

Sales

Public relations

Politics

Law

Corrections

Military personnel

Chapter 7: Empaths, Love & Sex

The Effects of an Intimate Relationship on an Empath

An empath in an intimate relationship for the first time might be shocked to find how invested they immediately are in the emotional wellbeing of the person in the relationship with them. They might find themselves alarmed at how in tune they are to those emotions, how much of their attention is taken up by that emotional energy, and they might have difficulty with keeping an appropriate amount of emotional distance between themselves and their partner in the beginning.

It can be hard for an empath to separate themselves from the things that are going on in the life of the other person, but they also might find that they have a hard time focusing on their own emotions, addressing their own needs, and doing the things that they need to do in order to live their life around this other person whose emotions now pervade all their mental space and dominate a large amount of their thinking.

However, someone who is empathic might find that they have a much better grasp on the whole relationship thing than they might have guessed, once they get a handle on separating their own emotions from those of their significant other.

Knowing when someone is upset without them having to tell you can do a lot to help you address that fact before it gets out of hand. Being an empath with emotional intelligence can allow you and your partner to speak very candidly about how you feel, why you feel the way you do, and how to address things moving forward.

This can cut out the cat and mouse game that can seem to manifest in the relationships of people who aren't really great for each other, who don't have emotional intelligence, and who can't seem to say what they mean, how they feel, or to discuss it in a way that can help bring them to a greater understanding.

Benefits of Empathy in an Intimate Relationship

Being empathetic in your relationship with other people gives you a much greater understanding of the person you're dating. Your empathic abilities give you a common ground to start on because you already understand how that person is feeling. This is a good deal of the fight when it comes to getting to know someone, so you're ahead of the game!

More and more people tend to relate to the more human aspects of their personalities as well. The things that make us anxious, the things that make us confused, and the things that just plain aren't fair. When we talk about these things and find common ground in dealing with this type of thing, it will give you something in common right from the jump.

Being an empath makes you more comfortable to be around and it makes it easier to relate to you on things. People will want to spend time with you and they will enjoy your company simply by virtue of your magnetism, your positive energy, and your empathic abilities.

Use that to your advantage to get comfortable with someone, to talk with them about the things that make them happy, and to establish a rapport with that person. Doing so gives you a great foundation for a relationship, as communication is such a key to successful ones.

When people say that communication is the key to successful relationships, this is because when you communicate effectively with someone, you are both putting your points of view out for each other to see, you discuss them, and you come to a mutual understanding that makes things go more smoothly.

This mutual understanding is predicated on that empathy that you can feel more strongly than other people around you can.

You can see their point of view much more easily, and that makes it so much easier for you to relate to that person. Use that to your advantage to create a healthy, happy relationship.

How to Manage Empathic Responses in a Relationship

One of the things you will need to do when you get into a relationship is to keep your empathic responses from telling you what the other person is trying to say before they say it. It is important to hear people out when they're talking to you and it's important to respond to what they're saying appropriately. If they feel like you're not listening to them, or that you don't want to hear all of what they have to say, they will take offense and it will be hard to mediate that and move forward from it. You cannot have effective communication if you're not doing your part of it.

Try not to fix your partner's feelings. If you find that your partner is having difficulty with something and you understand what the problem is, try not to fix it for them. There is nothing wrong with talking to someone who wants your input on the things they're going through, offering advice when they want it, and hearing what they have to say about everything that they're currently dealing with.

Do not, however, tell them how they are feeling, try to impose the solutions for those feelings, or interject yourself into the middle of the situation if you have not been asked to do so.

Furthermore, if you have asked how your partner is doing and they don't feel like talking to you about it, don't push them to do so. Don't ask your partner to share things with you when they're not comfortable doing so, no matter how well you think you understand what they're going through.

Someone coming to you about something they're going through should be done on their own cognizance, should be done with their willingness, and should be done so when they feel comfortable with it.

You cannot force someone to be comfortable, especially when they're not doing well. If your partner never gets comfortable in talking to you about their emotions, that will be an issue that you should address with them when they're doing well and when they have the emotional energy to hear you tell them such things.

Deep Personal Connections & Their Effects on Sex

Being an empath in a relationship with someone, you will often find that you have created an emotional connection with that person that is deeper than most that your partner has felt anywhere else. You will find that those connections affect every aspect of your life with that person, not the least of which is sex.

Feeling completely in tune with a person's emotional and physical responses makes the things that you say and do together bear a lot more weight than they ever would with other people. If you and your partner say, "I love you," it's not something that is out of habit and it will often bear a lot more weight than if you were to say it to someone who you love, but who doesn't share that same deep, emotional connection that the two of you share.

When having sexual relations with someone, being able to anticipate their needs, being able to tell how they feel, and being able to do things that intensify those feelings make those relations much more meaningful, and much more profound.

In short, sex with someone when you feel completely in love with them will always feel far better than sex you can have with someone who has a basic emotional connection with you. That deep emotional connection is tied to every single aspect of your lives together and it shows in everything you do.

Chapter 8: How to Overcome Anxiety & Fears

The Effects of Fear & Anxiety on the Body & Mind

Headaches

These can come and go, they can range in severity, and they can ruin your entire day. If you spend a lot of time stressing, there are things it can cause you to do that can cause a headache, or it can simply cause a headache on its own.

Make sure, if you're getting stress headaches, you're drinking plenty of water and that you're doing your best to get an appropriate amount of sleep at night. Eliminating screens before bedtime should also assist with the trouble of sleeping and headaches.

Muscle aches

Being stressed or anxious means that you're always tense. Thanks to this, your poor muscles can be exhausted before you even realize that you've been flexing them on a nearly constant basis.

These aches can occur all over the body from the calves and thighs, all the way up to the neck and face. These can be alleviated through massage, Epsom salt baths, supplements, and intake of calcium and magnesium in healthy dosages.

Chest pain

Being anxious can cause tightness in the chest. If the anxiety is strong enough, this can make you feel like you're having a cardiac episode, especially if you've never had a cardiac episode and all you know is that chest pain equals a cardiac episode. These can sometimes be accompanied by an elevated heart rate, sweating, heavy breathing, and other symptoms.

However, if you find that you're having chest pains while you're simply sitting there thinking about things and no other symptoms follow, look to the coping strategies in this book and put some of them to work for you.

IF YOU BELIEVE YOU'RE HAVING A CARDIAC EPISODE, CALL EMERGENCY SERVICES.

Fatigue

Because of how tense you are from stress and anxiety, all your physical energy has been spent and put into exhibiting the symptoms of stress and anxiety. It has overspent your physical and your emotional energy, so now you're sitting at a deficit, which makes you feel complete fatigue in both your mind and your body.

Loss of Sex Drive

It can be really difficult to feel the drive to do anything intimate or romantic when you're so preoccupied with feeling like everything is going badly. If you experience a loss in sex drive, you may want to consult with your physician. Many people only experience this symptom after many of the others have come to pass, and it's time to speak with a professional.

This might not be something that is of great importance to you in life, but it should be noted that if it was important to you at one time before things seemed to get more complicated, there is a chance that it is a symptom of anxiety or stress.

Upset Stomach

Being stressed can give you a case of the gurgles and it can give you a wicked stomachache or put your stomach in knots. Try to drink some water, eat something mild, and see how you feel. If you feel like you need to guzzle Pepto so you don't feel nauseated, you may want to speak with a professional.

Digestive Issues

If those stomach issues go unchecked, you might find that some more severe symptoms develop. Those knots in your stomach can lead to poor digestion, which can lead to irritable or irregular bowel function.

You may also find that the stress you've been feeling has elevated the acid production in your stomach. This acid production and stress can cause ulcers and other severe issues within the stomach.

Take care of yourself and, if you find that your stomach is getting holes in it because of all the stress and anxiety you're feeling, take proactive steps to make changes!

Sleep Problems

Proper rest is so important to living a good life, lowering stress, lowering anxiety, and getting through one's day with as little difficulty as possible. It's hard for your brain to manage everything that it needs to manage if you're not giving it the sleep it needs.

This is only exacerbated if you're also not eating properly, so both should be done in proper measure.

Be sure that you're not sleeping too little, or too much. You should be getting between six and eight hours of sleep per night, and you should be staying asleep through the night with the exception of a bathroom break or two.

If you're having trouble with this, speak with your doctor about what can be done to help you to get the sleep that is appropriate for you.

Rashes

Itchy or blotchy rashes on your skin can manifest if you're too stressed for too long. Hives are a common symptom of stress, but they should be addressed by a doctor. Scratching at those rashes in your skin can lead to skin tearing, infection, scarring, or worse.

Consult with a doctor about the best method of addressing those rashes, of returning your skin to normal, and of addressing the stress and the anxiety that helped those rashes to form in the first place.

Irregular Heartbeat

This is a very severe symptom and should be addressed by a medical professional. It may or may not be something that is permanent, but a doctor should be the one to tell you this for certain.

If you find that your fitness tracker or your own monitoring of your heartbeat is telling you that your heartbeat is behaving erratically, let your physician know, have them check you out, let them know what's been causing you stress lately, and ask for help with managing that symptom.

High Blood Pressure

Stress can cause your blood pressure to spike. As you're pushing to get things done, as you're worrying about things, and as you're imagining the worst-case scenarios while in the throes of anxiety and stress, your heart is working overtime. Your ticker is pumping the best is can and your blood pressure may raise while all this is going on as a result of that stress and anxiety.

Take steps to lower your blood pressure if you find that it's elevated. Improve your diet, reduce stress, get proper sleep, and speak with your doctor about the possibility of needing medication to lower it.

Odd Skin Dryness or Maladies

Psoriasis and eczema can occur in the skin if stress and anxiety go unaddressed. These are similar to rashes, but the condition will often require a steroid or special ointment to clear up properly. Thanks to these conditions being itchy, it's possible to open the skin with scratching and open you up to infections and scarring without proper treatment.

Be sure to speak with your doctor if you're exhibiting symptoms of stress-induced psoriasis or eczema.

Brittle, Lifeless, or Dull Hair

Thanks to all the other things that can come from stress and anxiety, it's possible for even your hair to show signs of it by going limp, looking frizzy, dull, or lifeless. You might find that your hair breaks much more easily, it never feels soft, it won't hold the style you want it to hold, and it won't hold color as well, either.

TMJ

TMJ is characterized by chronic pain or spasms in the jaw joint just near your ears. It can swell, it can throb, it can spasm, and it never feels great. TMJ can cause migraines and headaches, and it can be caused by a number of other health conditions. If you have TMJ and you are severely stressed, speak with your doctor to see if the two could possibly be connected.

Teeth Grinding

Gritting your teeth and grinding your jaws together when you're stressed can cause a lot of pain in the mouth and jaw. It can cause severe headaches, cracked teeth, and a lot of other problems in the body that you might not expect.

If you're grinding your teeth in your sleep, your doctor can prescribe a rubber guard to place between your teeth while you sleep at night to stop it from happening. The best option, however, is to address that stress that keeps you grinding your teeth day and night.

Your dentist won't thank you, but your teeth will!

Lowered Immune Response

When you are dealing with a lot of stress and anxiety, you might find that you get sick with much more frequency. You might find that you are susceptible to every cold that goes around the office, you might find that you get every little big that goes around, every stomachache, etc. This is due to the lowered immune response that your body has in times of extreme stress.

If you find that you are stressing out about things on a consistent basis, your body is expending a lot of additional energy that it likely doesn't have. One of the systems that the body has to pull energy from in order to use its other necessary functions, is the immune system.

Mood Swings

When we're stressed, we are much more likely to snap at the people around us, to feel a very small reprieve from moments that should make us happy, and to feel sad at the smallest little trigger. Thanks to these things, it can seem like we're wearing a new mood every 30 seconds throughout the day, when the fact is that we don't have the emotional energy to sustain anyone emotion for very long or to keep every negative emotional response at bay while we deal with everything that's going on in our lives.

Panic Attacks

Panic attacks, if you've never had one, are *nasty*. They are alarming, they feel terrible, and they give you the feeling that everything is crumbling around you. I promise you, this is not the case, you will be okay, you will survive the attack, and they do not last forever.

They are usually characterized by erratic breathing, sometimes hyperventilation, shaking, crying, a sense of doom, increased heart rate, and an inability to focus on things without being overwhelmed by them.

They will generally blow over in a matter of minutes, but they feel like they take forever when you're in the middle of them.

Depression

Being stressed over an extended period of time can leave you feeling like there just isn't any hope. Stress serves to make you feel like the things that aren't going well in your life are going to continue going badly and like there isn't anything you can do about them.

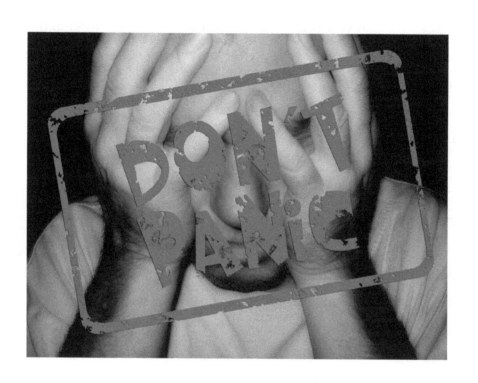

This is not the case, there is help to be had, and in many cases, there are physical things that you can do to make the changes that you need to make in how you're doing.

The coping strategies in this chapter will help you to make those changes, to manage your time properly, and to come back from the stress that your life puts on you from day to day.

If you feel like you might need to speak with a professional to change the way your stress and anxiety make you feel, then feel free to do so and get the help that you need.

Irritability

When you're in the middle of dealing with stress and anxiety, it can feel like any little annoyance that crosses your path is something that deserves the full weight of your wrath.

Being cranky as a result of stress is a response as old as stress itself. It doesn't make it okay, it doesn't make it less upsetting for the person on the receiving end, but it does help to know that you're not the only one who can react in this type of manner when things aren't going the way you feel they ought to be going.

Difficulty Breathing

Shortness of breath and hyperventilation can both cause huge problems for you. The biggest thing they're good for right off the bat is making your anxiety even worse. A few things can elevate your heart rate in the same way that not being able to breathe properly can do.

Focus on the controlled breathing exercises in the first part of the next section, even out your air intake, calm yourself down, and know that it will all be okay.

If you feel like you are suffocating or not getting enough air, have someone contact emergency services right away, as that could be something else. While you wait for them to arrive, just focus on your breathing and try to even it out.

Exhaustion

Between spending more energy than you have, poor sleeping, and everything else that stress and anxiety cause you to deal with throughout your daily life, there's really no wonder why you would feel completely exhausted by the end of each week.

Not being able to relax because of the stress and anxiety that you're feeling can cause you to get very little out of the time you're not spending at work. You don't feel like you're relaxing, and it might feel like you've just worked a 30-hour day!

Irregular Sweating Patterns

Sweating too much from palms, underarms, or the forehead when you're nervous is not uncommon. It can be embarrassing, but just remember that everything will be okay, drink plenty of cool water, replenish your electrolytes, and try to put yourself in a space with a lower temperature.

Don't fan yourself, as you will only serve to raise your body temperature and make the sweating worse!

Jumpiness

People who are frazzled or stressed beyond belief will often jump just about sky-high when startled. You might find that you're incredibly tense, waiting for something to go wrong or to happen, and the second it does, all your stress responses flash and you nearly leap out of your skin.

Dry Mouth

This can happen when you're stressed or anxious. Drink plenty of water, but don't drink too fast. You don't want that sloshing feeling in your belly when you're trying to deal with the things that are causing that stress.

Coping Strategies

Controlled Breathing

The first exercise we'll cover is called Natural Breathing. This is breathing that is focused on the abdominal region of your body. This exercise is one that can be adopted as your general manner of breathing throughout every day unless you're doing some sort of physical activity that exerts the body. By utilizing this practice throughout your day, your body will get the oxygen it needs, and exhalation of carbon dioxide will be closely regulated where it ought to be.

As you utilize this method, you will be slowly taking in a normal amount of air through your nose until your lungs are filled, then exhale evenly. The first time you give this a shot, you might want to put one hand on your stomach, as well as one on your chest. This will allow you to feel that the hand on your stomach will rise while the one on your chest stays level. This is your indication that you're breathing with the lower part of your lungs. As you continue to focus on this even rhythm of breathing, a sense of calm should begin to take over.

Natural Breathing

1. Place one hand on your stomach and one hand on your chest.

2. With a gentle and slow rhythm, inhale a normal, comfortable amount of air in through your nose, taking care to fill only your lower lungs. This means that the hand on your stomach should rise, while the hand on your chest remains level.

3. Exhale without much force, just allowing the breath to leave your body.

4. Continue breathing in this way with a relaxed approach, concentrating on your breath and not the things that have bothered you.

This pattern is sort of the stark contrast to the reflexive response of hyperventilating or breathing too fast and too shallowly to do the body any good in times of stress.

The second breathing technique is a more calming breath that sort of takes the reins, takes over your thinking, and stops the hyperventilation in its tracks. This is a great tactic to use in times when you're feeling a sense of panic or heavy anxiety. This method of breathing is one of the quicker ways to rein in hyperventilation and to bring you back around to that calmer, more collected frame of mind and physical state.

Calming Breathing

1. Place one hand on your stomach and one hand on your chest.
2. Through your nose, take a long, slow breath to fill your lower lungs first, then your upper lungs. You'll feel your hand on your stomach rise, then the hand on your chest.
3. To the count of three, hold your breath.
4. Through a small opening in your lips, slowly release the breath and feel the muscles relax in your chest and abdomen.
5. Relax the muscles in your face, jaw, and your shoulders to relieve stress and pressure.

In addition to being a great tactic for releasing you from the grips of hyperventilation, this is a great exercise that can help you to exercise calmness throughout your day. At several points when it's convenient for you, take the time to do this exercise. You can do this in times when tension rises, when work gets stressful, or even when you simply have a moment to yourself.

This exercise can be a great way to become comfortable and familiar with this process so that, in the event that you find yourself hyperventilating due to anxiety or stress, you will have this tactic under your belt and ready to use to bring you back around to even ground.

The more familiar you get yourself with this process during times of calm, the more readily you will be able to remember and use it during times of panic or high tension. Waiting for an emergency to strike before you prepare for it will set you up for a much more difficult time getting through it.

Question the Thought Pattern

Ask yourself if you're in the middle of a negative thought pattern that could be destructive to you if you continue on with it. As yourself if the thought pattern is one that is helpful or if it's one that is harmful. Is it one that should be permitted to continue because it will lead you to a better result, or is it one that will only hurt you if it's allowed to continue?

Simply by questioning the type of thought pattern you're dealing with, you interrupt it. Interrupting your thought pattern is the best starting point for changing its course and putting your mind onto a track that will yield better results.

Aromatherapy

Between incense, candles, essential oils and so many other means, there is no shortage of ways to introduce aromas into your life that will help you to feel less stressed, to feel happy, and to get some quality relaxation time into your day.

Take a little bit of time and breathe in those smells, close your eyes, and allow yourself to take the time to get the benefits from those aromas. Aromatherapy can be a hobby in its own right if you're interested in making candles, blending essential oils, and more.

Take a Walk

Taking a walk is a great exercise because it's light, it doesn't exhaust you, it gives you time to think, it gives you fresh air, and it gives you just a little burst of endorphins that you can use to help you get through periods of stress, sadness, anxiety, or other negative emotions.

Bonus points if you take your walk right after a meal, as this helps with digestion in the evenings and can lead to a much more sound and restful sleep!

Do Yoga

Yoga can help to relax you, to stretch you out, to keep you from being tense, and to center your mind. If you don't like doing the classroom thing, there are plenty of instructional videos and publications that will teach you how to do the poses in the comfort of your own home.

It is recommended that you try your poses with someone who knows how to teach them the first time around, so they can tell you if the things that you're doing are proper form, or if you need to adjust for safety.

Write it Out

No matter what you're feeling, you can always write it down to process it. You can even type it out if that is something you prefer to do to save paper, your hand muscles, and time. Going through your emotions at the pace it takes to write them out can help you to go through all the parts of what you're feeling, lay them out in a way that makes sense, and to understand the ramifications of everything you're dealing with.

Light Stretching and Muscle Relaxation

If you're feeling stressed or anxious, take some time to loosen all your muscles. Relax your shoulders, unclench your jaw, sit up straight, unclench your hips or glutes, and just let the muscles fall into a more comfortable position. Stretch your arms and joints light until you feel just slightly rubbery, then allow yourself to get back into your work once you're feeling better

Oxytocin Pressure Point

There is a pressure point in your hand, just between the thumb and forefinger that will release oxytocin when pressed. Without exerting so much pressure you hurt yourself, grip the thicker, soft flesh between your thumb and finger with the opposing thumb and forefinger, and press.

Do this for a few seconds while breathing deeply and slowly, then refocus on what you're doing. You should feel a little bit of relief.

Adjust Your Posture

Check the way you're sitting in your chair or standing at your desk. If you find yourself hunching over or in an odd position, make adjustments so you're sitting up straight, your chin is parallel to the desk surface, and your arms aren't extended too far from your body in order to complete your tasks.

Relax your muscles and get back to it.

Spend Time in Nature

Taking a walk along a body of water, spending time in the woods, or spending time with animals is a great way to bring yourself back down to Earth, so to speak. It can be so easy to get so tied up in the things that we need to do each day that we simply forget how the world around us.

People who are highly sensitive will generally find the properties of nature to be very restorative and will find a good deal of peace for them in the great outdoors.

Cope with the Hypothetical Worst-Case Scenario

If something, in particular, is worrying you, think about what the worst possible outcome for it could be. Tell yourself that this is simply an exercise in the hypothetical, that none of it will come to pass in the immediate term, and try to think about all the aspects of that outcome that would negatively affect you.

How could you cope with those things? What things would you do to bring your life back into the realm of normalcy and regularity? Could you do it?

Often, showing ourselves that we will be okay in any possible event is the way to cool down the anxiety response. Things will turn out okay and you will be fine.

Take a Break to Center Yourself

For some, this could mean a brief meditation. For others, this could simply mean pulling yourself out of whatever thought process has your brain all wrapped up, coming into the here and now, and working on the situation that is currently in front of you.

Once you feel that your attention has pulled away from that other situation that isn't right in front of you, go back into the tasks that need your immediate attention with all the attention you now have.

You will find things to go along much more smoothly when you make this effort and when you are very purposeful about what you do with all the attention you have to offer.

Take a Hot Bath

This one might sound cliché to you, but it's miraculous how much this can do. It's a very relaxing environment that you make for yourself when you take a bath, the water is very warm and relaxing, and you can add things to the water like bath bombs, Epsom salts, essential oils (make sure they're fit for skin contact), and more to help you relax and enjoy while you recuperate and recover with the help of the warmth and the additives in the water.

Organize Something

For some, the act of putting an organized system into their life, work, computer, or other places can help to bring a sense of calm into things. Organization makes things easier to deal with, easier to look at, easier to think about, and it can give one a sense of control and stability that they may not have previously had.

If you're feeling very anxious and aren't sure you have the ability to do very much to organize, take a small project and tackle that first. The drawer in the kitchen with all the random things in it that doesn't even open properly could probably use some help. Take all the old duck sauce packets and take out menus out of there and toss those because you likely don't need them. Put all the hardware and tools on one side, all the batteries on the other, and soon enough you'll find that you can actually see what's in the drawer when you open it!

This is a small task that gives you a rather notable sense of accomplishment! This accomplishment will help you to feel less anxiety, will help you to have the strength to get to the other things that you want to do, and will give you the confidence to tackle other organization projects with excitement.

Forgive Yourself

If you're feeling anxious about something that you've done improperly, inappropriately, or wrongly, then you need to forgive yourself. You are human, mistakes happen, lapses in judgment happen, and you don't deserve to be on the cross for whatever it was that you did.

If you hurt someone, apologize. If you did something that was wrong, do what you can to make it right. If you made a mistake, get help to fix it. This is all anyone can ask of you and it's all that you should ask of yourself.

If whatever has been done cannot be made right, do the best you can. Offer what help you can, make an effort to make a difference, and move on. You are human and, like the rest of us, you're going to make more mistakes. This is not the end of you.

Turn off the News

Watching the news or reading newspapers with regularity and impart a feeling of hopelessness into one's daily life. The way to keep one from feeling this hopelessness is to turn off the news and to get involved in local efforts to improve the status quo. Be nice to the people in your area, help to feel the homeless, talk to people about what is going well in their lives, compliment a stranger, pay for someone's coffee, or spend time in a coffee shop and watch how kind strangers are to one another.

This will help with the feeling of hopelessness. There are things that are not right in this world, there are people who do not get what they need, there are people who do things they shouldn't be doing, and there is always bad news to spread in the world, but your focus is what matters.

The things you focus on are the things that will dominate your life, so stay informed of the things that are important, but know that there is good in the world and do your best to contribute to it.

Make a List of Things That You've Been Avoiding and Do One of Them

Sometimes, we can get overwhelmed by the list of things that we've been putting off for quite some time. Renew your registration, call your mother, write that email to your kid's teacher, or whatever else there is on your list that you need to get done.

Don't feel bad, we all have things that we've put onto the back burner while more important things were getting done in our lives. The important thing is that we get these things done before they cause a problem and that we don't allow them to cause us anxiety.

Once they're done, you will likely feel a purge of anxiety that is stronger than you expected. These tiny little tasks can tie up so much more of our attention and our emotional energy than we generally tend to realize.

Clean Something You've Been Meaning to Clean

When was the last time you scrubbed around the rim of the tub? Is it getting grimy? You might do well to do things of this type, as it alleviates a lot of pressure to do so. This can be the inside of the fridge, your credit report, your living room, that one closet that the kids know never to open unless they want the house to flood with junk, the basement, the car, or even the kids' rooms.

These things being cluttered can actually take up space in our minds. It eats up the mental energy we have for certain things, it makes us anxious, and we just hate looking at it! Not to mention how we feel when someone important comes over (read: mother-in-law) and almost opens the closet.

Do yourself a favor and dedicate a couple of hours a week to cleaning out those areas and you will see at the end of them how much good it will do for you to see these things improve right before your eyes.

Mindfulness

Mindfulness can be done mentally, but it can also be done on paper. If you like the concept of mindfulness, and you like the concept of writing down your feelings, try writing your mindfulness thought processes in a journal.

This provides a record of how you're feeling from day to day, and it will also tell you if you're consistently getting a good result from your meditation.

Meditation

Meditation has a large number of variations, types, and focuses. It's possible that one type of meditation does nothing for you while another type does everything for you, so be sure to look around. Find a method that works for you and take time to let go of the things in your day that has the potential to keep you from getting the rest you need for the next day.

If You've Been Reading Too Much into a Subject, Stop

While it is prudent for us to look into the things that are causing us difficulty in life, or into the things we wish to achieve, things that help with work, and so much more, there is such a thing as too much of a good thing. It is possible to do so much research into a topic that we get over-informed and we start to develop anxiety about it.

This is not necessary, and it can actually do more to set us back than it can to give us the leg up that we need in order to succeed. There is nothing wrong with being informed, just stay balanced.

If You've Made a Mistake That Is Bothering You, Make a Positive Step Toward Avoiding It in the Future

It's possible with anxiety, to think of something we've done that was not correct or proper, and then to completely agonize over it. This can happen in spite of the issue being so small someone likely didn't even notice it happened.

If you messed up on something, no matter how big or small it is, all you can do it take steps to make it right. Worrying about it isn't something that will help to remedy the problem, the people in your environment won't benefit from you agonizing over it, and you won't get over it if you keep worrying about it in that manner.

Ask Yourself If You're Being Overly Dramatic

Stop yourself in the thought process that is making you feel bad. Ask yourself if you're thinking of things in balance, or if you're being a tad overdramatic about the impact of the things you're thinking about.

For instance, it's a common saying that one wants to crawl into a hole and die when one does something embarrassing like asking someone when their baby is due when they're not pregnant. It's rude, it comes across terribly, and it's horribly embarrassing. However, it's not worth dying over, it's not worth agonizing over.

You said you were sorry as soon as it happened, you excused yourself from the area, and you made it very clear that you were only trying to be friendly before you put your foot in your mouth. The person that you asked will likely think it's funny that it happened and will probably move on in a very short order.

All you need to do is ask yourself if the response of crawling into a hole and dying about it is an appropriate one. The answer will always be no, and you can lower your anxiety level about it. Then laugh at yourself because it's hilarious, mistakes happen, and then move on!

Examine Triggers

Knowing the things that cause us to feel sad, stressed, or anxious can help us to avoid those things in the future. When you're feeling anxious, asking yourself what it is that made you feel that way is a great way to backtrack and to isolate how to move forward in your life without getting tripped up by those types of situations in the future.

For instance, if you know that you get anxious whenever someone talks about a particular subject, you know that you can either steer the conversation away from that topic, or you can excuse yourself from the group while they have that discussion without you.

If You're Comparing Your Situation to Someone Else's, Stop

Comparing your own situations to someone else's in life is a terrible way to live. It's the fastest way to make yourself feel bad about where you are in life, to invalidate the progress that you've made, to lessen the efforts that you make, and it's also a really inaccurate representation of what the other person's situation is.

You don't know what the other person put into their situation, you don't know how long it took them to get to that point, you don't know how hard it was for them to do all that, and you don't know if the situation is really as perfect as it may seem from an outside view. Perspective is everything.

If you must make a comparison, compare how you are currently doing with how you were previously doing. Are you better off now than you were a year ago? Are you happier than you were a year ago? What changed?

You're doing great and the fact that you're putting the work into your life to improve it means so much.

Make a To-Do List for Your Day and Do the Easiest Thing on It

Making a to-do list is a great way to know what's ahead of you in the day, it can help you to block out your time properly, and it helps you to make sure you don't miss anything when you're going through all the various things in your day.

When you make your list, if you're feeling anxious, go ahead and knock off the easiest thing on your list. This will give you a sense of accomplishment, make your list look smaller, and will keep you going onto the next thing! This is a tactic I use at work, at home, in school, with the kids, and with every project I work on personally.

Slow Down

If you're feeling very anxious about a deadline or about a task that you're currently doing, chances are that you're probably going a little bit faster than you really need to. Working at the fastest pace possible can burn you out before you get through the rest of the things you need to do today, and it can cause unnecessary tension and raised blood pressure.

Just pull back for a moment, breathe deeply, and adjust your pace so you're working evenly and at a pace that is sustainable. There is nothing wrong with working at a pace that ensures you will finish your work by your deadline, but you will rarely need to work yourself to death over a deadline!

Ask Someone About a Time They Were Nervous and Have Them Tell You How It Turned Out

It can be very helpful to find out that someone we admire a great deal has struggled with the same feelings that we're struggling with. As someone whose opinion you value to tell you about a situation that made them nervous, what happened in that situation, and how it turned out.

Generally, you will find that the situation went well, the results were positive, and that they felt silly for even worrying in the first place. While you're not comparing your scenarios, it can help to know that the vast majority of nervousness felt in the world leads up to a very anti-climactic result of smooth success.

Distract Yourself for a Bit

If you're feeling too anxious to continue working on something, allow yourself to get pulled into something else that is unrelated. Feel free to set a time frame for this so you don't fall too far behind but taking some time away from the task at hand can ease some of the anxiety a bit.

This will allow you to come back to the things you need to do with a refreshed mindset, with a zeal for completing what you need to complete, and with a clear head.

Allow Yourself to Enjoy Things

There is a fairly common response to anxiety that people have, which is to deny ourselves the things that make us happy because of our shortcomings and our minor failings. We tell ourselves that because we failed at one thing or another, or because we didn't do something quite the way we wanted to or in the time frame that we had hoped we would, that we don't deserve to go out and enjoy a movie with our friends. We tell ourselves that we should have to work several hours late because of these things, we tell ourselves that we need to cancel trips we're taking to see family, or worse.

The truth is that you don't deserve to lose when you make mistakes. You deserve to do better next time because you learned from the mistake that you made.

Laugh

Laughter is the best medicine! Laughing makes you feel happy, safe, and it is good for your health. It can help you let go of some of the anxiety you may be feeling in life, and it lets you let loose in a way that so few other things do.

Make sure that you're spending time with people who make you laugh, people that will laugh with you, and laugh as much as you can! If your face hurts from all the laughing by the time you're done spending time with that person, then you've picked a good one!

Watch television and movies that make you laugh, talk about dumb things with your friends, tell jokes, read funny articles, look at funny pictures, and laugh as often as you can because it will make you feel so much better than you might even realize.

Lightly Run Your Fingers over the Lips to Activate the Parasympathetic Fibers in Them

Similar to the acupressure point in your hand, running your fingers lightly over your lips can activate the parasympathetic fibers in them that will make you feel much calmer. Doing this idly while you research things, while you work on the computer, while you read, or while you're watching television can help you to relax a little more fully.

This isn't something will stop an anxiety attack in its tracks or anything, but it is something that can make relaxing a little bit more effective and enjoyable.

If a Situation Is Causing You Anxiety, Think About It from the Vantage Point of Six Months in the Future. What About It Still Matters?

Some of the things that keep us worried are things that are not particularly relevant. If something isn't going to matter in six months, you might not need to be as worried about it as you currently are. You might find that you could let go of some of the things causing you to worry in life at the moment if you know it will be fine.

If you're preparing a party for a friend and you're trying to get the streamers twisted in a pattern that looks right, but they won't cooperate, is it worth being anxious or stressed? Is the person you're throwing the party for going to be paying attention to the number of twists in the party streamers and whether or not it was even on both sides?

Spend your time focusing on the things that matter, and not the things that make you anxious because those things won't matter in six months. What will matter in six months is if you're still feeling so anxious and your blood pressure is raised because of silly little things like party streamers.

You are more important than party streamers.

Connect with a Friend

Sometimes, all it takes to set us back onto the right path and to keep us level is connecting with someone whose company we enjoy. It doesn't necessarily have to mean that we talk with that friend about the things that are making us anxious. It doesn't mean that we have to have them tell us it will be okay. It just means spending time with them. Laughing about silly stuff, hearing about what they're working on in their free time, playing board games together, or going out and having fun.

Never underestimate the value of human connection, of relating to people on a personal level, of talking about nothing, of playing games with people we enjoy, and of having adventures!

Imagine One Positive Outcome for Every Negative One That You've Thought Of

If you find yourself coming up with countless negative possibilities for a situation that is making you nervous, sit down and think up one positive outcome for each negative one that has occurred to you. Think of every possible thing that could go right with this situation that has presented itself to you.

This exercise is useful because, after some time, it will start to become second nature to do this automatically. Every time something comes up as a possibly bad outcome, then you will think of something that could go well. Over time, you will focus more on the positive than the negative and you will notice a shift in the tone of your thought process.

If There Are Any Two-Minute Items on Your To-Do List for the Day, Go Ahead and Get Them Done

If you can think of some things that you need to do with your week or your day that will take two minutes or so, go ahead and knock those out. This will mark off so many things in your week that you will have to get done and it will clear up so much space in your mind.

You won't be struggling to remember all the things that you need to do throughout your week, you'll have long stretches of time to devote to the things that are more important or more involved on your to-do list, and this will cut down on so much anxiety.

You would be shocked to find how much of your anxiety is linked to all the little things.

Try a New Exercise

Lookup a new type of exercise, a new stretch, yoga position, or something similar that interests you and give it a whirl! If you totally stink at it, you can work on it over time and get better at it. If you are a total natural, then that's something to be proud of!

Spending time doing new exercises and fun physical activities is a great thing to spend your spare time on because it gives you more physical energy, it gives you endorphins, it makes you feel good physically, and it gives you time to think. Work it out!

Accept What You Cannot Change

There will always be things in life that we cannot change. We can't change the weather, we can't change the location of states, we can't change how long the wait is at the DMV. The things that we can change give us power, but they also place a burden of responsibility on us.

If we know and accept the things that we cannot change, this frees up that responsibility and allows us to place it on the things that we can change. Be willing to accept that certain things are the way they are and think about the things that you can affect aside from that, and work within the parameters that leave you.

Allow Yourself to Relax

If you're trying to take a bath, watch a movie, spend time with friends, lie down, or relax in some other way and you continue to find yourself checking your work email, looking for texts from other parents in the scouts troop, or checking your credit report, then you're not really allowing yourself to relax. You're looking for more things that will keep you busy and will keep your mind engaged.

Put the phone away, do the things that you know relax you, enjoy them, allow yourself to recover from the day you've had, and focus on creating more emotional energy for the day you will have tomorrow.

Eat Well

COFFEE IS NOT A MEAL. All too often, people who are exceedingly busy will find themselves swinging through the coffee shop for a latte and allowing themselves to start their day on nothing but cream, sugar, and caffeine. This is not a way to live, it's not a way to reduce anxiety, and it's not helpful to your body in any measure.

You need to eat balanced meals throughout the day that provide you both with the carbohydrates, protein, and fat that it needs to create energy and to do all the things that it does for you every day.

Do your body a favor and remember your food groups, of which coffee is not one!

Sleep Well

Proper rest is so important to living a good life, lowering stress, lowering anxiety, and getting through one's day with as little difficulty as possible. It's hard for your brain to manage everything that it needs to manage if you're not giving it the sleep it needs.

This is only exacerbated if you're also not eating properly, so both should be done in proper measure.

Be sure that you're not sleeping too little, or too much. You should be getting between six and eight hours of sleep per night, and you should be staying asleep through the night with the exception of a bathroom break or two.

If you're having trouble with this, speak with your doctor about what can be done to help you to get the sleep that is appropriate for you.

Exercise Proper Time Management

Managing your time should be a priority, as it allows you to fit everything into your day that you might need to get done. If you spend all of your time on one task and then find, at the end of the day, that you had about six tasks to do, you will find yourself feeling anxious or pressed for time.

If you're able to budget out your time and work on the things you would like to get done, then keep your time managed so everything is taken care of over the course of your day, then you will have a much easier time with getting everything completed in the time that it should be done.

Surround Yourself with People You Like

Life is too short to spend it with people that annoy you, right? People that you don't like, who annoy you, who set your teeth on edge, or who just make you uncomfortable will raise your stress level. You cannot fully relax around people like that and you cannot spend your whole life without relaxing.

Choose friends that make you feel good about yourself, friends who make you laugh, friends who appreciate your dorkiest qualities, and friends who encourage you. People who do these things for you and expect it in return are valuable friends that will help you to grow, be yourself, and will lower your stress and anxiety levels.

Spend Time with People You Love

People you love will often inspire you to be relaxed, will help you to feel happy, will release chemicals in your brain that make you happy, and they will often help you to bear the burdens that you have in life. People who love you are people who want to see you succeed and they're people who should get a lot of your time in life.

Spending all your time with people who upset you, people who don't deserve your time, with work that stresses you out, with stupid annoyances that cause you stress, and with tasks that bring you no joy will make your life seem like it's not very worth living.

Spending your time with the people you love, doing things that you love to do, having experiences you want to have, eating food you want to eat, and just being happy are the things that make life worth living. Live the life you want to live and spend your time with the people that you love.

Spend Time on Your Hobbies

Hobbies are so important. They can even you out, help you to decompress after a long day, can give your mind a place to escape to, and they often allow you to come out of it with something that you've created as a result of your personal time or skill investment!

Pick some of the things from this section that really speak to you and implement them into your life. Write down which things you're doing, how you feel as a result of them, and weed out the ones that don't help. Stick with the ones that make life even more worth living.

Conclusion

Thank you for making it through to the end *of The Empath Survival Guide: The Complete Strategies for Highly Sensitive People. How to Learn to Manage your Emotions, Overcome Anxiety and Fears, Learn Protection Techniques from Energy Vampires*! Let's hope it was informative and able to provide you with all of the tools you need to achieve your goals whatever they may be.

If you haven't done so already, your next step is to make use of the techniques laid out in each chapter to help you to understand the mechanisms at work in your life. They will help you to find healthy coping strategies and will help you to heal from past traumas or incidents.

Thank you very much for reading and please share the information you found helpful with friends and family who may also benefit. Finally, if you found this book useful in any way, a review on Amazon is always appreciated!

CPSIA information can be obtained
at www.ICGtesting.com
Printed in the USA
LVHW042022201020
669278LV00005B/705